From "Hero" to Zero and Back!

Lessons from a Veteran's Civilian Employment Experience

Steve Speakes

Army Veteran, 1974-2009
Businessman, 2010- Present

*The term "hero" is used sardonically, as I'm not calling myself a "hero", and instead using the term to compare my start point with the fall that happened in my first civilian job experience.

Copyright 2017 by Stephen M Speakes

Use or distribution in any and all forms prohibited without express permission of the author.

This book is dedicated to the nameless and largely invisible Veterans who return home to the Nation they have served so faithfully after their military careers end. When they return, they find to their surprise that the citizens they left behind have no sight of them. So it is up to each Veteran to reconnect and find their own fulfillment and value following their Service careers. It is to help them, and spare them some of the pain I have experienced in my journey, that this book is dedicated.

Sincerely,
Steve Speakes
Army Veteran
San Antonio, Texas
January, 2018

Executive Summary

This is the story of one of the 50,000+ Veterans annually* who retire from the military and transition to civilian life, many of whom will attempt new careers in commercial management positions. Following 35 years in the Army, I reflect on my seven years as a civilian businessman to compare the two environments and share lessons learned.

When I was let go from my first civilian job I began a thoughtful assessment of how to become more successful moving forward. I believe that while Service retirees have much to provide, they also have more to learn before they can parlay their time in uniform into successful civilian careers.

I liken the preparation process to how the military has learned to prepare for counter insurgency warfare, emphasizing long term full spectrum operations rather than swift and violent engagements. I will discuss how to frame the choice for a new life, then how to prepare for a strong civilian career. The journey continues by providing better awareness on the complexities of joining a large, modern company and how to interact, communicate, and organize with new associates.

I conclude by providing a vision of a strong transition program linking legendary military values to newly honed skills and self-awareness to shape success. A civilian reader committed to supporting fellow citizens in the transition process will also be empowered by a candid look at the capabilities, needs, vulnerabilities, and expectations of a newly retired military leader.

---

* Department of Defense, Office of the Actuary, Number of Military Retirees Receiving Retired Pay by Year, 1900 – Present, September 30, 2015.

Table of Contents

1. Introduction 3
2. Decision Point 11
3. On Boarding 23
4. Decoding Your New Team and Teammates........ 33
5. Building Your Toolkit 41
6. Strengthening Your Business Skills.............. 47
7. Experiencing Failure and Recovering............ 51
8. Concluding Thoughts 57

    Appendices 63
       a. Career Planning Checklists
       b. Your Resume
       c. Tips for Success
       d. Glossary

Introduction

"Good Morning Steve. I called you in to let you know that we no longer need your services."

Biographical Sketch

I began my career as an Armor officer and served the early years in traditional command and staff assignments in the US and Europe. I married in my first assignment and we were quickly blessed with twin sons. Our family learned to love the Army so we never seriously considered leaving the Service. My sons were at Texas A&M when the invasion of Iraq happened in 2003 and our family was based at nearby Fort Hood, Texas. I deployed as a part of the 4th Infantry Division to Iraq as an assistant division commander. Reassigned in theater, I flew to Kuwait to serve as the deputy commander responsible for theater logistics for another year. During this period my wife remained at Ft. Hood and our sons entered the Army as armor officers heading for Iraq.

In 2004, I was posted to the Pentagon where I would remain until I retired in 2009. In Washington I assumed responsibility for "equipping the Army" as the director of force development. I went on to become the Army's deputy chief of staff for programs, or G8, responsible for the Army's financial strategy.

On retirement, we returned to Texas where I became an executive vice president for strategy and transformation at USAA. When that job ended, I became the president and CEO of Kalmar Rough Terrain Center, a DoD contractor known for making the RT240 rough terrain container handler. After seven years as a civilian it's time to share my reflections on transitioning with other retiring military leaders.

Hitting Bottom

One Monday morning three years into my new career I received a surprise call to see my boss immediately. My curiosity was heightened because he lived by a strict schedule and this was a departure from the ordinary. With some anxiety, I walked in to the office and heard words I'll never forget.

"Good Morning Steve, I called you in to let you know that we no longer need your services."

I was overcome with surprise, fear, and embarrassment; his face swirled in front of me like an image going down a drain. I fought for control, listened to the rest of what he said and then walked unsteadily out of his office. As I emerged it seemed that everybody was looking at me with strange new eyes — I was now a failure for the first time.

Returning to my office I called my wife and told her "Dear, I was just fired…" So, after decades in the Military and three years trying to "make it" in the civilian world, this was the result? Yes.

> But getting fired in your first job should not be a prerequisite to success.

This story is written to help you avoid crashing like I did. Was this result entirely a surprise? No, of course not. Could I have made better choices to make myself successful? Certainly. Upon reflection, my primary shortcomings should have been obvious to me (and others) when I was hired. They led directly to my failure. Correcting them has been essential to my current success as a CEO in business.

But getting fired in your first job should not be a prerequisite to success. This is what I failed to do the first time around:

- Understand what was expected of me.
- Know the technical aspects of the business well enough to operate professionally.
- Find a genuine mentor and develop strong relationships with my new associates.
- Collaborate with my peers and direct reports.
- Improve my communication skills (particularly listening and non-verbal skills).
- Learn the culture and the pace of the corporate processes.
- Read the career warning signs and navigate through performance issues.

So, let's learn from my two experiences in the corporate world and seven years as a civilian what I should have known when I started this new journey as a civilian. My intent is NOT to discourage you from attempting the transition from wearing a uniform to becoming a member of a corporate management team. Your success in a variety of assignments over many years argues strongly that you can adapt and become extremely successful in the corporate world. Over the course of the past seven years I have found the challenge of growing new skills and developing a new value proposition for myself incredibly exciting and fulfilling. As Veterans we must commit to rebuild our skills and to study to enable our great qualities to shine.

We have many shining examples of successful transitions. However, they may blind us to the rough moments that occur even in successful transitions. A number of successful examples do not negate the need for careful study before you embark on the journey. The lessons I learned are not universal. I do not think they are as applicable in a smaller, more entrepreneurial opportunity. I also do not believe that "all companies are alike." Cultures vary greatly. I have tried to compare my experience with other retirees and Veterans to see if there is commonality. There appears to be considerable similarity.

After reading this you may be better equipped to anticipate how your behavior may impact others in the commercial environment. I also believe that the more a senior military leader relied on the authority that accompanied his position to make decisions and influence others, the ruder the awakening will be on entering the private sector. Conversely, a staff officer who is accustomed to leading via consensus and using relationships and persuasion to get things done is probably much better positioned for the transition.

> My intent is NOT to discourage you from attempting the transition from wearing a uniform to becoming a member of a corporate management team.

My focus is assisting senior military leaders (officers and senior non-commissioned officers) to successfully transition to the civilian world after military careers. There is commonality in our experience that is worth sharing regardless of how long we served, what Service we were in, and what rank we attained. It often is a largely solitary experience compared to our previous entry into the military as a year group or class. We must recognize that our military training and career experience has forever changed us, and in fact may betray us by tempting us to use the wrong techniques and skills for our new environment.

To prepare you for my approach, review your memories of our military in Iraq. We began with a strategy that headlined "shock and awe" as the keys to success. Over time we learned the value of a counter insurgency strategy. The focus on firepower and swift, overwhelming victory diminished as we learned how to utilize the full set of skills to achieve success over a multi-year campaign. We learned to prepare and study for each deployment, to fully understand the area of operations in all of its dimensions to set conditions for long term success.

Pause to consider this admonition from "Lawrence of Arabia" drawn from the US Army's web page on Counter Insurgency (COIN) warfare:

> T.E Lawrence attributed his success in aiding the Arab Revolt against the Ottoman Empire to "hard study and brain-work and concentration," an example at odds with what he denounced as the "fundamental, crippling, incuriousness" of many fellow officers who were "too much body and too little head." Future combat leaders should heed Lawrence's injunction to study hard, especially when preparing for COIN – the most intellectually challenging realm of warfare.

If we replace the word "COIN" with "your first civilian employment" in the line above we have a shared understanding of the hard study needed to be successful in making the transition. Your considerable military skills, ethics and devotion to duty can be the foundation of a magnificent second career. However, if used inappropriately they may set conditions for failure just as "shock and awe" failed over time when not supplemented by a long-term strategy for full spectrum success. In the pages ahead, you will be prepared for your "next deployment" to exploit your strengths and minimize your weaknesses. "Hard study" will be essential and above all you must be curious and observant in your new operating environment.

Decision Point

We all come to a point where our first act ends and yet the show must go on.

In my case I liken the last years of my Army career to that of an aging NFL place kicker. I remained on the team roster, still went to team meetings, and was able to stand on the sidelines with the team during games, but I was under no delusions. I was no longer truly a warrior preparing for deployments and sharing the risks of being a Soldier. While I still felt the thrill of putting on a uniform every day

> When you realize that the end has come – and it happens to all of us – our future is shaped by action or by default.

I realized that I was no longer contributing like the brave young men and women who went back and forth to war. Finally, one day, just like every player in pro sports you realize (or are forced to accept) that the time has come and the dream must end. You have been (or soon will be) waived from the team! You are still relatively young, but the precise skill set honed over years in the military no longer guarantees instant acceptance in your new world.

When you realize that the end has come – and it happens to all of us – our future is shaped by action or by default. I chose a path of action, studying those that went before me and seeking out the advice of civilians I came in contact with.

Shaping your "new life" will be a profoundly challenging experience. Success requires great honesty with yourself and your family. Choices such as where to live, what income goals to set, and what opportunities to pursue all require serious reflection and prioritization.

My path resulted from several personal decisions. My wife wanted to come back to Texas, so that meant not pursuing the familiar Washington, DC environment. I wanted to join a new team, learn new skills, and not rely on my last Army positions to land a business development opportunity. Yet, each person's journey is personal and to be successful must result from honest self-reflection and prioritization as we will discuss in the next chapter.

I thought that because I had been on the Army's corporate staff my skill set would facilitate my transition. I also wanted to move quickly from the Army to my next job, reasoning that this would minimize time spent in limbo and

> What I did not understand was the toll that the Army had taken on me personally and my family and how little I was intellectually, emotionally, and physically ready to move forward.

lost opportunities to pursue unique jobs.

What I did not understand was the toll that the Army had taken on me personally and on my family, and *how little I was intellectually, emotionally, and physically ready to move forward.*

The Way Forward

As you begin preparing for your new life, pause and reflect on how your military career has shaped you differently than others who have spent their lives in the commercial world. Let's examine the direct value of your qualifications as a Veteran by comparing the military environment with the characteristics of the commercial world. You will need to sharpen your Priority Intelligence Requirements (PIR) for this new theater of operations. To bridge the gap between previous experience and the future, three topics key to making a successful transition will be addressed: a new organizational construct, different relationships, and unique decision-making patterns.

> To bridge the gap between previous experience and the future, three topics key to making a successful transition will be addressed: a new organizational construct, different relationships, and unique decision-making patterns.

After that we will hone practical skills so you will be able to perceive your new world with greater acuity. Next, we will review the technical business skills used in daily life by a successful corporate manager. If despite these lessons, you are let go, it is crucial that the termination be discussed so you can deal with it and move on. Finally, let's apply what you have learned and describe success. You do have great skills, and like the US military over the past decades you can reshape your identity. (For those readers who are corporate leaders, recruiters, or HR managers, consider using these thoughts to shape your organization for successful Veteran transitions).

Two Worlds

Let's challenge the assertion that Veterans are ideally suited by military experience to reenter the job market with skills and abilities directly suited to the business world. In our hearts we know that cannot be completely true.

From Hero to Zero and Back!

Unlike the post-World War II era, military experience is not a common thread in our culture. Instead, as the 1% in our population that has donned a uniform we have developed very specialized skills in a very unique culture. Throughout our careers as service members we have prized the qualities and characteristics which make us different. In many instances they were essential to advancement in the military. Now they may be counterproductive to your corporate success.

> In my case the transition was the most difficult challenge of my life.

As a group we share special ethics. In basic training, we were "broken" from our past identities and learned a new one. That new identity recognizes rank, understands its meaning in terms of certification, education, experience and respect. With increasing rank comes age, so we tend to be most comfortable with "mature" leaders. We believe that regardless of background, opportunity is widely (if not universally) available in our ranks and we rely on our comrades. We share confidences, and trust one another intuitively.

Military organizations are defined by hierarchy and operate within it. Individual roles are understood by all and job-defined authority is respected. Prior to decision-making, discussion or debate is often focused and free. During this phase, opinions and options are sharply defined and clearly delineated. Then, debate stops as choices are made and orders are given to be obeyed with strict timelines. Whether we have been directly in combat or not, we have been totally dependent on others. Trust is assumed. Teams are made and remade on an annual basis. Few deployable organizations and daily work relationships last longer than an annual cycle.

The reality of decades of continuous conflict has shown that failure and delay results in lost lives. We are impatient with process that appears slow and bureaucratic. We demand results now and expect others to understand lessons learned as immediate operative guidance. If these are our shared experiences and common beliefs, how do they mesh with "the real world" we are entering? They don't. Our worlds are far apart and much like the story of Americans and Brits separated by a "common" language, so Veterans are separated from their fellow citizens by life changing different experiences. As a Veteran striving to survive and prosper in the commercial world we must understand how distinct our experience and instincts are and how they imperil our prospects of a smooth and successful post military transition.

We also should recognize that as civilians very few of us are selected for employment directly for what we "were" in the military. We must make a transition well beyond trading a uniform for civilian garb. The comparatively rare exceptions to this rule are flag or general officers and senior non-commissioned officers who serve on corporate boards or as consultants. In those rare cases, the Veteran can keep his/her title and military approach as a civilian because that is why they were hired. To their new employers, they represent military thinking and values. Adding complexity to our challenge is the common belief we share as veterans. Leaders in the military are not prepared to start over at the bottom. Instead, we believe that our development and success in the military qualifies us to avoid entering the civilian world at the bottom of the pyramid and starting over.

We believe in the strength of our real-world experience and people skills, while not understanding the magnitude of our shortcomings in technical knowledge, interpersonal skills, and background that comes from years spent pursuing a civilian profession. Many Veterans' self-belief is so strong that they don't question the assumption that they are entitled to make a jump from one management position in our profession to another. Were we to reverse this assumption we might better see the arrogance or naiveté of our ways.

How would we feel if the executive officer of a ship, a battalion, or a squadron gained lateral entry from the commercial world and was selected for that role based on a strong interview, and equivalent years of exemplary experience in a major corporation? Once we recovered from our amazement and likely resentment, could we develop a way to bridge the experience and cultural gap to help the newly appointed officer achieve success? Would we welcome him or her if the job they were given was one for which we had applied? Hold that comparison in mind during your transition to help you understand how your new colleagues are relating to you.

In my case the transition was the most difficult challenge of my life. To be successful we must develop a new identity and skills which differ radically from what we have been. Adopting this new identity also means that in many cases we must alter or abandon the very skills and techniques that made us successful in our previous life. Can an "old dog learn new tricks?" The answer in your case must be "yes" to survive in your strange new world.

Decision Point

Making the decision to transition to another way of life from the Military is an extraordinarily difficult experience. Other military leaders whom I have tried to help with the process often stop me by asking, "How did you get there?" "How did you get started?" They wanted to know what series of events or choices landed me in a management position with a large commercial enterprise.

Self-Assessment
For me the transition began with the assumption of my final Army assignment. As I began this last job I knew I was not destined for further promotion and began thinking about my next step.

First, I had to accept reality – the end of a great profession was near. I started talking to those either in transition or already in post-military employment. I also sought personal relationships with those outside of the Army. To do so I sought to move beyond business and share social experiences (lunches, dinners) with those I met while on the job. Breaking down the barriers of position and rank takes time and effort, but was well worth it.

As time went on I began to evaluate the choices for my "next life". A good friend identified options in broad terms – working simply for money, choosing work because of location, or for passion. As I went forward I developed a slightly more sophisticated set of choices:
- How hard do I want to work?
- Do I want to retain my military identity or reinvent myself outside of the DoD environment?
- Are my values most naturally in harmony with charity, volunteer work, or commercial success?

- Do I want to work independently or as a member of a team?
- Where do I want to live?
- What is important to my family?
- How important is earning additional income?
- What are my peers who have already transitioned from military to civilian life doing and are they enjoying it?

As we begin this self-evaluation, honesty is vital. While some may disparage a career focused on earning potential, it is a perfectly legitimate choice depending on your needs. Anyone wanting to buy a home, send children to college while trying to live on a military pension will likely find dollars in short supply. But simply choosing a new career for the money blinds us to accompanying burdens that often sour the deal. I hope that after reading this you will be more aware of the baggage that often accompanies a path into the world of corporations and large institutions.

> But simply choosing a new career for the money blinds us to accompanying burdens that often sour the deal.

I began my journey with what I thought was a reasonable amount of humility in regard to my talents and likeability. And my instinct was that if something special was going to be mine, I had to work for it. So, I set my sights on the following:

Goals

I wanted to work aggressively to land a position in executive management of a large company. I would work hard; earn respect as a Veteran who learned new skills and a sense of value in a new line of work. My wife and I wanted to return to Texas if possible. I felt that earning additional income was important to supplement my military retirement in the lifestyle that we wanted for ourselves. Once you have made some decisions about how you want to structure your new life, tell people about it – friends, close relatives, recent retirees, business associates. The point is to advertise your availability. Word of mouth referrals are the best way to gain opportunities and you should make sure that everyone in your network is aware of your goals and timeline for achieving them.

When I retired, two companies in defense industry were interested in hiring me, but they wanted me to work in "business development," pursuing and increasing their government business. When I asked if their career development plan enabled me to "graduate" from business development (a staff position) to running a business they said it was not in the cards.

Even for people like me, who had operated on the business side of the Army's corporate headquarters, there was little to no opportunity to move into more standard management positions. One other opportunity quickly captured my interest. A Fortune 150 firm serving the military was seeking senior level retirees for new positions in corporate management. This promised to be more than business development and it was in Texas!

The Recruiter

Suddenly, I was brought into the processes of a major corporate recruiter. For all of us who have done little or no preparation for job selection process, this is a huge change. The first thing to understand as a transitioning Veteran is that the corporate recruiter is working for "them" – the firm or organization that is doing the hiring – not you. They are paid when one of their candidates is hired by their client. My experience with two major recruiting firms showed that their methods are very similar.

The Process

Interaction begins when you either hear about a job and contact the recruiter or a friend or a colleague recommends you to the recruiter. If possible, get the job specifications before calling the recruiter. Read them carefully. Though they may sound very stylized, they are written to tell the discerning candidate a great deal about the job. Key things you want to learn from the job description:
- How is the job defined?
- Where is the job?
- What qualifications do they establish?
- Who will you work for?
- Is the job a developmental opportunity?
- How does the firm describe themselves and their hiring goals?

Immediately learn as much as you can about the company if their identity is disclosed in the job description (sometimes masked by generic terms like "a large US firm with annual revenues of $620M with offices located in the southeast US is seeking a leader to run their combat systems business").

If they have divulged their identity, read their website. Contact any friends you know who work or have worked for them. Read about them on social media. If they are publicly traded, read their most recent corporate report (found on their website under "investor relations"). The purpose of this advance work is to learn as much as you can before speaking with the recruiter. If you do not know the firm, then you must learn as much about them as possible from the recruiter. Listen very carefully the first time you and the recruiter speak. Take notes and have your questions ready. If the recruiter decides that you are worthy of follow-up, there will be a formal interview with the recruiter. Prepare carefully using the job description, qualifications and qualities they identified as important in their job description. Have your questions ready. As the candidate you should view it as your job to have prepared your discussion points and questions in writing and available to you during the interview.

> Prepare carefully using the job description, qualifications and qualities they identified as important in their job description.

Your goals from this initial meeting should focus in the following areas:

- What is the job (is there an overriding need that has been given the recruiter)?
- What can the recruiter tell you about "the unspoken intent" of his client that he has not put in writing? (For example, do they want to round out their executive team with a person with a specific background)?
- What are the most important attributes they are looking for?
- Where is the job located?
- What is the hiring process?
- Who will you report to?
- When are they making their selection?
- Are there any significant issues the job entails, such as continuous travel?

The hiring process normally involves screening by the talent firm to provide the corporation a "slate" of potential candidates for possible hire. They begin by studying your resume, reviewing your references and conducting basic background checks. The next phase should be a meeting with the firm that is hiring. When you meet with representatives of the company, study the interview list carefully. Ideally the group should include your potential boss, peers, at least one person who will directly report to you as well as a representative from HR.

Use all the tools at your disposal – including "Linked In" – to learn about the people you will meet. Each of them is likely assigned a primary objective in your interview. My experience is that typical corporate interviews are fair and to the point (not dominated by trick questions).

Interviewers will focus on what they think are the skills and attributes most critical to making the right selection for the job. If they have a technical or performance issue they need to solve, questions will revolve around how you can help. If they have concern about your ability to be a good cultural fit, you can be sure they will ask leading questions to see how you think and how you work with others.

> You need practice in anticipating the nature of the questions and responding in terms that will be perceived as value added and strong cultural fits. Take advantage of your mentor to help you to prepare.

You need practice in anticipating the nature of the questions and responding in terms that will be perceived as value added and strong cultural fits. Take advantage of your mentor to help you to prepare. (Ideally your mentor is someone in the company or a related company to the one you are interviewing for).

Use one of the many standard hiring guide books to prepare and better anticipate the generic questions you can expect. Successive interviews are physically and emotionally demanding. You are on the center stage and everybody is evaluating you. (Practical hint: If an executive assistant is leading you from office to office do not be surprised if he/she is asked for an opinion about you, so treat every interaction as a potential interview).

Do not interview without adequate time to rest and prepare. If you can't give the process the required amount of preparation then you are

not ready to pursue the position. First impressions are overwhelmingly important and in most cases irreversible. I found my "interview days" were demanding emotionally, mentally, and physically. When your interviews conclude, sit down as soon as possible and make notes about the experience for each person who questioned you.
- What did they ask?
- How do you grade yourself?
- Where did you shine?
- Where were you weak?

When your personal After Action Review (AAR) is complete, you should make contact with your recruiter. He/she wants to understand how you believed the interviews went compared with what the company HR rep has said.

Your self-awareness is important. If you are able to anticipate questions the company may have about you based on the interviews be sure to answer those questions for the recruiter. Your recruiter may be able to provide your perspective on why you fumbled a question. Conversely, if you felt very comfortable about your ability in a key area, it's good to say so. It helps to put an exclamation mark on your strengths and qualifications for the job.

> Do not interview without adequate time to rest and prepare.

Sometime before or after "final interviews" you may be asked to perform in a simulated job environment. I have been through two of these. For a transitioning Servicemember, I think they are exceptionally difficult because they assume you are already a professional in their world. Job simulations often begin with an innocent sounding e-mail directing you to a website. There, you find a great deal of information about an imaginary company and position similar to the job you are competing for. You will be given recent annual reports of the company, fictitious descriptions about your future associates and a heads-up about issues you must be ready to address on your first day of work. As a non-MBA graduate I found my first such experience overwhelming. The complexity of the material provided – annual reports, business forecasts and anticipated strategy – challenged my ability to answer questions pertinent to my "first day" on the job.

To prepare, I asked for help from friends who had MBAs and were in business. They were instrumental in prepping me to perform on

From Hero to Zero and Back!

the hypothetical first day of work. As the day unfolded, it resembled a military operational readiness test. "Stuff" happened every hour of the six-hour experience to test the candidate in a variety of ways. Because I was prepared when I arrived the day was fun, but arriving unprepared would have been a disaster. To be ready, I undertook a full weekend of study. While your technical abilities to understand business reporting and scenarios are tested in this scenario, the real objective of the event is to evaluate your ability to interact with potential superiors, peers, and direct reports.

You must solve problems in a practical, common sense way. The people you interact with are role players trained to evaluate you from a psychological perspective. At the conclusion of the day you will be given an AAR with one or more of the staff. In this AAR they will be looking to see if you have enough self-awareness to tell them where you struggled and where you performed well. Be modest!

> Your self-awareness is important.

Reflections on the process

In the preceding paragraphs we sped through the job "courtship" process. Imagine that following a casual referral by a friend, you met the recruiter and things went well. Suddenly things can move beyond your control very quickly. This argues that before you test the job market you must think carefully. Let's examine some thoughts and activities you might want to reflect on before you begin.

Start time

There are varying opinions about when you should start engaging potential employers. If you are still in the military, the first person you should consult is your ethics adviser. Be confident you understand the ground rules regarding who you can talk with and to what extent before you get into moral, ethical, and potentially legal gray areas.

In some cases, while you are still in your DoD job you can "recuse" yourself from any involvement with a potential future employer, but obviously, this limits your effectiveness in that position. Once you are comfortable with the complexities of the transition, be conscious of differences between

> Suddenly things can move beyond your control very quickly.

> Be confident you understand the ground rules regarding who you can talk with and to what extent before you get into moral, ethical, and potentially legal gray areas.

your military experience and your new work environment. In the commercial world there typically is not an annual replacement cycle like in the military. Instead, jobs come available in an unplanned and unpredictable manner. If you are still on active duty this can present a quandary as you see the "perfect job" open and close while you remain bound to the service.

Having navigated the legal quagmires associated with seeking your next employment, you have other issues to address. Think carefully about when you want to have more than an introductory, informal conversation with a potential employer. Getting caught up in the job search process can quickly become all-consuming. You may decide you will wait until after your retirement to do this. While that choice eliminates most of the ethical challenges and preparation of doing this while on active duty, it is not without risk and consequences. Like many of us, you may be living in government quarters and be faced with an immediate choice about where to live in the interlude. When you enter retirement, you become a resident of a state and assume all the accompanying tax burdens while you simultaneously adjusting to living on 50-60% of your recent pay and benefits.

A Pause

If you choose not to attempt both your military job and a job search you may find yourself in limbo between active duty and your first job as a civilian. Most of us do not take "real vacations" in our final jobs in the military. Now is your chance. Put your stuff in storage. Make a long overdue investment in your family. See the things that you have always wanted to see. Get some real rest.

Attend to any health issues you have been ignoring. Take some time to reflect on your personal values and priorities without being short on sleep and time. Become reacquainted with your family. This break from the bedlam of a high stress life might be your first opportunity to get to know yourself again, as well as the values and priorities of your family. When I was considering

> I strongly recommend some "down time" as you depart the military.

this option, I heard that the longer we remain unemployed following retirement, the more our economic worth goes down. For a reasonable period (six to eighteen months) nothing could be more untrue. You have earned the right to a pause and people will respect that. Once your regeneration process has run its course, you will have plenty of time to get back into the "market". I strongly recommend some "down time" as you depart the military.

Your Qualifications

The one document you should take proper time and care with is your resume. Too often we assume that it is a mere formality. Do not simply take a "good looking" resume from a friend and copy it, inserting descriptions that apply to you in place of your friend. You should not do this anymore than you would borrow a friend's clothes just because the outfit carried the day at their interview.

View your resume as the document that introduces YOU to THEM. It's your declaration regarding who you are; your strengths, desires, and background. When you invest the time to write your own resume – and not simply crib it from a "template" – you find that a proper introduction of who you truly are has been made.

People will make choices about whether to interview you based on your resume. Describe yourself as you want to be known. There are many good books on how to write a resume. Scan a few. Decide what process works best for you and devote a weekend to writing your own resume. Be careful to use terms understood by your audience. Describe yourself in accurate terms that will be useful to your audience. The people doing the hiring should not have to parse your self-description to place you in the job they have in mind.

> View your resume as the document that introduces YOU to THEM.

If you are/or and want to be a supply chain expert, say so. If you are a process engineer, do the same. Usually we err in the other direction by indicating that we can "do anything" and call ourselves "an operations leader" or some other quasi-military generic description. Examine the phrase at the top of the resume that you have used to characterize yourself. When you say you are a "results oriented," "innovative" and "collaborative" leader what have you really said about yourself that is useful? Not much.

Often, it's useful to think about tailoring your resume for individual opportunities. Some organizations are intimately familiar with "military speak" and are comfortable with DoD acronyms. Others are not. Look at the job description of the job you are interested in. Do you align with what they are expecting? I have frequently tailored my resume to fit the customer while preserving the essentials of who I am and what I can offer. So can you.

Once you have a draft, give it to your mentors and listen to their feedback. Everybody has a different opinion about what is good or not in a resume. It's your story, so consider the feedback but the final decisions are yours. (In an appendix to this guide I have provided additional thoughts on resume preparation).

> If you were like me, you were skinny and scared.

As you finalize your resume, review and update your existing professional "social media" presence or start one. *Facebook* is not considered a professional business site, whereas *Linked In* is. Hard work in preparing a useful resume will pay off as you begin building your *Linked In* profile.

The Interview

There are as many interview styles as there are companies; no single generalization is accurate. But, there are general guidelines and in this section, we will discuss some.

Remember the day you entered the Service? If you were like me, you were skinny and scared. That is not a bad mental framework to adopt as you prepare for post-military interviews. Like that time in your youth, you should feel some anxiety. You should feel lean and hungry and determined to learn this new game. But you have a lot to learn.

So far, you have done a lot to tilt the odds in your favor. You studied the company, its history, its recent performance, learned about its leadership and culture. You almost have the job description memorized.

On social media, you have looked up the people who will be interviewing you. Where possible, you learned something about their families, hobbies, and background to anticipate how their lives might tie into your own.

If they have written a blog, article, or given a speech, you know about it. You have thought through how your unique skills and qualifications can make their organization better. You are rested, and you are wearing clothes consistent with the advice given by the Company's HR representative. (Ask if this is not mentioned).

Sadly, not all of us follow these seemingly obvious cues. Some among us mistakenly assume that our past reputation will qualify us for the job and that the interview is just a formality. They will probably be disappointed.

I mentioned that there are no "do overs" in the hiring process. When we fail, we are out. If you get a candid debrief on why you failed, listen carefully for issues of culture and preparation. If they perceived that you did not take the trouble to learn about the company, could not relate to them, or were unable to persuade them of your value – that is why you failed. And if you were successful enough to move to the next round of interviews, you should still ask if there were any concerns you might address to make you a stronger candidate.

Let's assume that you get the needed feedback from the recruiter. You then expect a reasonably prompt response from the company about the job. They might, for example, schedule another round of interviews, or conduct further screening.

> "... you are using a watch to tell time; they are using a calendar!"

In your mind "reasonable" probably means "a few days". Get rid of that thought immediately. The best counsel I received while waiting for a hiring decision was from a friend who said, "Relax, Steve, you are using a watch to tell time; they are using a calendar!"

Typically, if a number of people interviewed you, each had to complete evaluations and turn them in to HR. That can take days or weeks. If you passed the first screening, HR usually convenes a meeting for all interviewers to share their impressions. Armed with the results, the hiring authority will make a decision. Simultaneously the HR team is likely doing a background investigation. All of it has to come together for them to make a decision. Nothing is easy or simple in the hiring process. You can ask for a timeline, but don't be surprised when it is not followed. Do not try to speed up the process. I can think of one reason for you to interrupt the process and talk to either the HR leader or your recruiter. It is to let them know you have received a competing offer, must make a decision, and would appreciate their decision if one is available.

On Boarding

Congratulations! You have successfully negotiated the hiring process and have just signed on to a new team! You are excited and ready to begin the next great adventure in your life. We want to identify what you should have derived from the interview and job search experience.

Derived knowledge
Think about the job.
- Is the position new to the organization? (Beware of a new position created just for you.)
- What happened to the previous occupant of your new position?
- Why did he or she leave?
- Do you have a clear understanding of who you are working for and what requirements await you?
- Are your new peers and direct reports ready for you to assume your role?
- Do you have a sponsor? Is that person responsible for making you successful?
- What technical and cultural training will you receive?
- What reputation does your new employer have on social media?
- What do Veterans' groups think about the company?

The purpose of these questions is to ensure you have done all the necessary homework to succeed. Just as your new prospective employer did their due diligence on you, you should have done the same on them.

> Just as your new prospective employer did their due diligence on you, you should have done the same on them.

You should be assessing them for a "mutual" fit. Use a website such as *glassdoor.com* to evaluate how the company's current or former employees feel about their employer. If the search leads to concerns or doubts, do not ignore them. Examine the interview schedule to make sure you have seen enough of the company to assess the company culture.

You need a good understanding of the organization and its culture to enhance your chances of success. Ideally you should meet potential direct reports, peers, and superiors as a part of the interview process. Use these opportunities to question your counterparts. Less than frank answers or encouraging responses are red flags.

When offered the job you have a final opportunity to make sure you are truly satisfied with the opportunity. If in doubt, proceed with caution! Time spent on this topic may be more useful to long-term happiness than focusing on negotiating your compensation.

Although the questions posed in the paragraph above seem innocent, they are not, and their negative implications are serious. For example:

- Your research indicated that Veterans you know or heard about had left the company after short stays.
- When you went for your interview and you asked about the job, you learned that the job was newly defined and brought together various organizations within the company into a new team.
- Performance expectations were vague and you sensed it would be up to you to help define them.
- Future peers you engaged in the interview process struggled to define specific expectations for the job or express genuine enthusiasm about it.
- When you recognized that you lacked the requisite technical knowledge to be fully successful in your new role, you asked about a training program. You learned the company expected you to "learn on the job" and there was no specific plan to help you ramp up.

Conclusions like the examples above should raise substantial concerns as you evaluate the job opportunity. Companies do have varying success with Veterans. That means something. Try to distinguish the success of entry level transitioning Veterans (versus senior level) to be sure they measure your probability of success.

> Companies do have varying success with Veterans.

Handing a Veteran an ill-defined job with little peer support and an unclear training program does not bode well for your survival. As the job seeker you must evaluate your opportunities with clear eyes and ensure you have made a good assessment of your challenges and chances. As a manager, I have seen sad failures by Veterans who – even with company and peer support – struggled. This is not a theoretical problem.

What You Bring to the Team

We think we bring an awesome set of skills to the corporate world. We have led teams to perform complex tasks on short notice, often without adequate technical training for the assigned task.

We thrive under pressure, believe that we have unique skills to reach out and motivate teams and are accustomed to change. The litany of stories – even by junior military leaders – who have assumed responsibility and done the unexpected expands our confidence. We did it once; we can do it again in the civilian world. Too often those experiences with "success" in executing unexpected and unfamiliar tasks give us misplaced confidence we will soon regret.

> If in doubt, proceed with caution!

I had run complex logistic operations in Southwest Asia, then moved to the Pentagon, learned how "to equip the Army," and finally how to plan and communicate the Army's financial strategy. I saw myself as a strong team builder, a quick study, an accepted member of a team of peers, a person who could quickly refocus an organization, and a strong communicator. My self-perception (or misperception) of my strengths accompanied me into the corporate world.

What I did not see were some very serious shortcomings in my skill set. Throughout my military career I had been in an incredible hurry and that pace intensified when the country went to war in 2001. As leaders at all levels we were routinely expected to perform instantly in a new assignment and implement changes to meet specific, highly dynamic job definitions. To meet those objectives, we specialized in

> What I did not see were some very serious shortcomings in my skill set.

a quick analysis of over-riding requirements, laser focus on building a strategy to meet the objectives, communicating the solution and then leading its execution.

When we encountered opposition to the solution, the combination of an abbreviated time frame and our position power often obviated the need to seek peer and subordinate agreement. As military leaders we seldom dealt with multi-generational communication customs. Our dealings were principally with subordinates, peers, and superiors largely of the same generation as we were.

This hid the complex challenge of dealing with different approaches to collaboration: processing information, seeking buy in, and gaining support while the concept was being developed. In a military world where orders are given and followed, I was somewhat blind to the weakness of this form of buy-in. It was also very difficult for me to understand how important technical mastery and operational experience are in the commercial world. Many years of intense study of the military arts had given me strengths I relied on throughout my career, but did not appreciate the difficulty of replicating similar skills as a civilian. Just like lieutenants in the Army, in corporate America, interns progress to become professionals through intensive technical study and years of experience performing fundamental business functions.

> When I arrived, I should have been more cautious and focused on analyzing the organization and building relationships before working to bring the "change" to the organization that I thought was my primary mission.

For me to think that I could parachute into "their" world and quickly absorb the necessary technical skills to complement the great executive skills I perceived myself to possess demonstrated an acute lack of self-awareness all the way around. When I arrived, I should have been more cautious and focused on analyzing the organization and building relationships before working to bring the "change" to the organization that I thought was my primary mission.

Whatever mismatch existed between my skills and those required was complicated by the perception many civilians have of us. New peers in the business world are outwardly welcoming, but can conceal real and legitimate reservations about our role. They may admire our dedication and sense of purpose, but have also seen our weaknesses – too many of us have had serious lapses in morals, language, and judgment once we become "civilians." In companies accustomed to cyclic hiring of former military leaders, they have seen us come and go with amazing speed.

Veterans are often too accustomed to large personal staffs and having things done for them that corporate or private sector peers routinely do for themselves. Our communication skills are often focused on transmitting rather than the cultivated art of listening. We are untrained in the subtlety of corporate communications, too often interpreting nuanced, but unmistakable dissent for thoughtful agreement. When a corporate colleague responds that he/she finds our idea "interesting" they are probably strongly disagreeing. In the corporate world – even down at the level of a small business, it is unlikely that anybody "rules".

> We are untrained in the subtlety of corporate communications

Even CEOs struggle diligently for consensus from direct reports. Corporate processes move by various patterns to achieve "alignment." Much like the United Nations Security Council, one negative vote from a powerful stakeholder can often torpedo an idea. More unusual to a military person, "decisions" are probably never final and are more likely iterative. This means that what you think you are bringing to the team is often not exactly what your new peers want. The initial impressions you make should be designed to allay these fears and emphasize your self-awareness and devotion to adapting rather than acting out the military stereotype.

Your new colleagues want to admire you and accept you, but you frankly come with baggage that dampens their enthusiasm for you. To be successful you must diminish or mitigate their anxiety, and work diligently to build up the skills that you lack. It is up to you to judge and prioritize whether your principal deficits are interpersonal or technical. Respect for the difficulty of achieving both should guide your early planning, priorities and activities.

Compensation and Benefits

Do not focus on the financial terms of the compensation to the exclusion of other compensation that in most cases matters more in

the long term. Despite the relentless discussion in various executive transition courses on bargaining for the "best deal," I suggest devoting more time to the non-monetary aspects of compensation. If you are signing on to a major firm they generally have established pay levels for various jobs. Ask them to explain the basis for their salary proposal:
- How is your job being categorized and why? (Jobs are developed for a specific level based on programmatic and/or supervisory responsibility, and seniority.)
- Are they using a local or national pay scale to establish your offer?
- At what level of peers' compensation are they benchmarking their salaries? (For example, some leading national firms will benchmark at 90% meaning that they intend for your pay to be equal to or better than 90% of the population. Others set more modest goals - - for example at 50%.)

Your efforts as a beginner to "negotiate" improvements to the offer may irritate people whose good will is essential to sponsoring you into the organization. You are not joining the NFL as a former college all-star. You're a mid-career player who did well in the Canadian Football League. You might be fast enough and strong enough to survive in the NFL, but you will have to learn quickly to prove you can stay.

> I suggest devoting more time to the non-monetary aspects of compensation.

As a boss in the commercial world when I hear that a Veteran who has been offered a job is displeased with our offer and is attempting to bargain, my reaction is frustration with little flexibility to give. Here is what is behind that mindset: As a Veteran you probably require longer than normal start up investments (on-boarding, orientation, technical training, among other things.) Therefore, you are something of an investment risk. Why complicate an already risky proposition by determined bargaining? While a "bargaining" candidate may get a trivial increase in salary or benefits, the long-term damage in terms of perception may outlive any short-term gains achieved. (You should use the Internet to do informal benchmarking to determine local pay levels and typical compensation for the position you are being considered for).

Understand what the corporate world terms your "total package" of compensation. Beyond base pay you want to know in detail:
- How are bonuses determined? Ask the HR team to show you with most recent company performance data how your bonus would translate to income.
- How much is in stock and how much is in cash?
- Will the company allow you to defer your bonus so you do not create a higher tax burden for yourself than necessary?
- Will your bonus "vest" (meaning become yours) even if you terminate your employment or are terminated?
- When can you retire from the company?
- What is the company's 401K plan and how does the company "match" employee contributions?

Honest answers to these questions are vital to your new financial survival. As a civilian you now have a host of new responsibilities: housing, possibly health care, and ever-rising state and local taxes. Finally, ask to see the company's personnel evaluation system. Your annual performance rating may help to determine your bonus eligibility, so it's good to know how that figures in.

> ...you will have to learn quickly to prove you can stay.

Many organizations have "centers of mass" for ratings just like the Service. This may have a great impact on your true bonus eligibility. For example, if the corporate center of mass is 3 out of a possible evaluation of 5 and it in turn caps your bonus eligibility at 50% then you can easily determine what your bonus would be. Having a general framework to evaluate all of these forms a key basis for subsequent or parallel decisions that you will make regarding housing and education and many other potentially negotiated compensation variables.

Day One

This is an experience you will likely never forget. Many of us started our military careers as teenagers or very young adults. Now you are making this first step into your new world as a "grownup". If you are honest you will feel the weight of your inexperience and be excited to prove your value as a civilian.

> If you pack your household goods prior to moving to the town of your new job, it is important to know the requirements for in-processing.

The company will have told you in advance what documentation is required on your first day. If you pack your household goods prior to moving to the town of your new job, it is important to know the requirements for in-processing. There is little flexibility to this. Most major companies do "batch" in-processing of newly arrived employees. You may be asked at in-processing to make decisions you were not prepared to make, so it's a great idea if you can have your HR representative provide you a guidebook ahead of time.

As a part of your in-processing you will acknowledge comprehension and compliance with company policy. In our new cyber-environment, the company may tell you that you will be subject to monitoring of your electronic media while you are "on campus" or when you use company equipment, such as computers and phones. Companies are also careful to safeguard their Intellectual Property (IP) and proprietary information even long after you have left the company.

> … companies may require even junior employees to sign confidentiality and "non-compete" agreements.

To protect their IP, companies may require even junior employees to sign confidentiality and "non-compete" agreements. This means you cannot work for a list of competitors defined by your company for a set period after you leave them (regardless of circumstance). You will also be asked to read and acknowledge pages of guidance explaining your obligation to safeguard their proprietary knowledge. When you agree to such an obligation you should note the requirement – either in a notebook or with a copy if you are allowed to have a copy.

They also want to ensure that if you have a dispute with them, they control your ability to take them to court. The assumption that as an American that you can tell anybody "I will see you in court" may be mistaken – you likely signed away your rights to do that. Companies employ a little-discussed method to limit your ability to litigate a personnel issue by having you sign an agreement to submit any disputes

From Hero to Zero and Back! 31

with the company to binding arbitration.

That means that the proceeding is confidential (meaning you can't talk about or publicize it). Lawyers will advise you that if you proceed with such a complaint you will pay for your own attorney and it could take as much as three years to resolve. If your experiences as an employee or the circumstances of potential departure appear unfair, be aware of the rights surrendered as a condition of employment.

> … any Veteran who assumes that he/she can disregard their employer's requirements does so at their peril.

The point of this summary of potential consequences of your "onboarding" is to make clear the importance of your agreement with the company. Violation of any of the requirements may be cause for termination. After years of following the Uniform Code of Military Justice (UCMJ), any Veteran who assumes that he/she can disregard their employer's requirements does so at their peril. If you have doubts regarding what you do with your Company's IP, ask in advance to safeguard your continued employment. Corporate espionage is real and just like our experiences in the military, violations can cost people their livelihoods.

Having negotiated these complexities, you survived in-processing and are now ready to join your private sector/corporate team.

Decoding Your New Team and Teammates

Organization

You come to your new civilian team with the best of intent. You believe that you have adequate skills to operate in an organization – really any organization because you have been in so many over the years.

I can still tell you that in July 1970 I joined the Army and became a proud member of 3rd Squad, 4th Platoon, 8th New Cadet Company, US Corps of Cadets at West Point, New York. I shared my life with fellow squad mates all day and most of the night. We were judged as a group, punished as a group, and rewarded as a group. We learned to collaborate with one another and to trust one another. We shared a squad leader, Mr. Schnabel, and he in turn reported to Mr. Holcomb, the platoon leader.

At the top of it all was General Walker, Commandant of Cadets. In some form, all of the organizations I was a part of over a 35-year military career had the same basic framework and the same sense of deep personal alignment. I bet that if we observed next summer's New Cadet Training at West Point the cadets would be assigned to structures very similar to my experience.

Which means that certain enduring military principles survive to this day unchanged: We knew who we worked for; our teams were clearly defined; loyalty was absolute, and friendships outside of our organization were secondary. We were focused on a common mission and shared a deep spiritual alignment. We learned to collaborate outside of our organizations as a secondary skill and not nearly as important as being a teammate. No unit I was ever a part of extended beyond 36 months. Annually, the Army scatters the pieces of its puzzle and builds

> ... there is nothing enduring about commercial business organizations.

new ones. As a result, longstanding personal loyalties matter much less because of the transitory nature of the military. Servicemembers affiliate quickly with their new teammates. We tend to commit fully to the team we are currently on. The mantra becomes to minimize the past and focus on the present. To illustrate the divergence of that lifestyle with a civilian bureaucracy looks at two paradigms.

On the right at the top is a standard organization chart and below it is a spider's web.

As Veterans, we associate with the "organization chart" and struggle to see the spider's web as a competing model. Why is the spider's web a better model for the Veteran's new work environment? Note the presence of both horizontal and vertical vectors in the web. Defining the boundaries of an organization in the web would be very difficult given the diffuse pattern of the web. This spreads responsibility across many organizations. Note the de-emphasis of hierarchy. From the center of the web, a leader could easily access any part of the web.

As a Soldier, this represents major change. My first loyalty beyond my immediate team was always vertical. In your new world it might be lateral. Note the difficulty of defining organizational echelons. We come from a world where strict hierarchy rules. That may not be the case where peer judgments and counsel may outweigh the impact of our actual boss. Finally, unlike the Napoleonic staff model (where functional responsibilities are delineated in enduring terms: e.g., the "3" does operations, the "4" does "logistics"), there is nothing enduring about commercial business organizations. They are constantly realigning and redefining themselves based on the needs of the then current businesses' and leaders' preferences. This year, a major company may have new layers, new bosses and new functions when compared to the previous year. Not surprisingly, what does not change are the people who do the work. Once you get to know them you will learn that even large companies reorganize

> Your natural instinct is to establish organizational boundaries, responsibilities, and align on with a new mission statement. In many cases, that is exactly the wrong thing to do.

What You Already Know

DIRECTOR
TOM

MAINTENANCE	SALES	PROJECT	
Erwin	Peter	Paul	
Gabor	Susy	Gabriel	Peter
Chris	Clark	Todd	Steve
George	Liz	John	Leslie
Veronica	Brown	Dave	Faith
Patricia	Fred	Gordon	Jeremy
Andy	Will	Gaby	Jason
Tim		Pete	

What You SHOULD Know

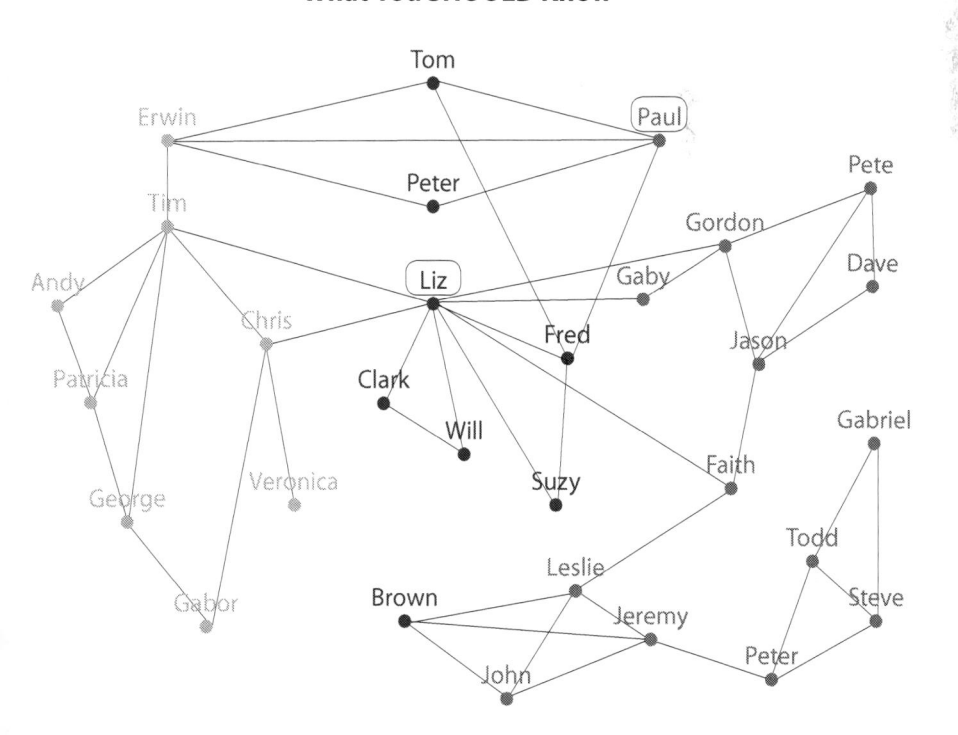

> I suggest Veterans now in the private sector "embrace the chaos" of their new team!

frequently but the individual employees remain in place under "change."

Many will tell you, "oh, yes, we tried that organizational construct five years ago. It did not work then, and it probably won't work now, but we will see…"

What else should the Veteran learn to guide his/her initial actions? I suggest that you not attempt to define or impose your organizational paradigm on your company's. Your natural instinct is to establish organizational boundaries, responsibilities, and align with a new mission statement. In many cases, that is exactly the wrong thing to do.

Your background in operational missions leads you to fix – or attempt to – decision-making, organization limits and boundaries. You know that when a Soldier must be resupplied in combat, or when artillery fire must be cleared there is no room for confusion. Thus, we eliminate diffuse responsibility and focus on precise organizational alignment. You are now in a very different world, and you must adapt.

I suggest Veterans now in the private sector "embrace the chaos" of their new team! I also recommend that they ignore years of training to impose order and not attempt to impose their definition of order on their strange new world upon arrival. A much more useful arrival technique is to dig in, study, and learn how it works. This is much less satisfying, but it is the true key to success in understanding the complex organizational and personal relationships guiding the conduct of business.

As a newcomer, several organizations may share a function in ways that completely confuse you. Months later you may concede that while the process is untidy, the result is good. And that is all that matters.

Focus a part of your initial meetings finding out from colleagues how you might best contribute to the organization. When I transitioned, I received ambivalent responses about what was expected of me. At the time, I did not understand the gravity of these words. What I now know is that doubt about my role would continue unless I could quickly establish value. These questions were never answered satisfactorily and contributed to why I was asked to leave. If you get strong encouragement to do something or fix something, follow it! Your

> …the commercial decision-making process operates in a culturally unique manner in each company.

colleague is telling you how you can not only survive but succeed. If you can figure out how to make positive contributions while adding value you will be highly prized in the business world. Also, study the pace of the organization. I made the transition in 2010 and was profoundly (and unknowingly) influenced by my recent past on Army Staff.

Back then, our decision-making process operated on a weekly basis from department headquarters to delivery of results to the Soldier on the ground. When I joined the civilian world, an unseen clock was already ticking in my mind. It took me too long to understand that the commercial decision-making process operates in a culturally unique manner in each company.

You may find that the biggest barrier to enacting timely change is the fear of acting. If things are going "pretty well" now, be absolutely sure you are improving what may already be a good state of affairs. Study your process; seek advice before acting, while respecting your colleagues and mutual need for collaboration in advance of a decision.

When an issue you have initiated and coordinated comes up for a decision, don't blame your colleagues when they express dissent. Blame yourself. Somehow, you violated organizational norms and did not realize it until the concerns were made public. Do not be amazed if some weeks or months later the decision is changed. As learning organizations many companies reverse ground on previous decisions quickly. Never assume action has been taken on an idea you have endorsed just because the topic was "decided".

> Make a major objective of seeking out and cultivating your own relationships.

Think of the relative freedom that many NFL quarterbacks have to "call an audible" after the quarterback gets behind the center, reviews the coverage and determines that the planned play will not work. It's often the same way "at the line of scrimmage" in the private sector.

Relationships

If learning to read your new organization is difficult, understanding the relationships that define your new team is doubly challenging. The most difficult part is they are unwritten and nearly impossible for a new arrival to decipher.

We have had huge advantages in the Military that enable us to quickly learn who works for whom: From rank we know seniority, from branch or service identification we know organizational specialty. When we review military bios, we learn when and where someone has served in combat and can guess who knows whom. In your new private-sector environment there is the same complexity, but much less transparency of your colleagues' backgrounds.

> When you socialize, avoid talking about your previous career and your past.

Make a major objective of seeking out and cultivating your own relationships. This is vital because unlike the military you probably share few if any long term friendships with your colleagues. As a senior leader in the military ask yourself how much time you focused on maintaining or establishing relationships. In my case very little time was spent doing that. My final years in the military were consumed with work and the demands of a schedule. Those whom I encountered on the job probably shared a previous assignment or a schooling experience. Even if we were not always friends, we were colleagues, and we did not need to devote much energy to establishing a basis for trust and dialogue. Things are different now. You are new and you are the stranger who came in from outside.

> To be successful in a management position you must hear what the rest of the tribe does.

Be observant and develop an appreciation for how people socialize. Some of your new friends will work out in the gym before work - a great place to transcend the formality of the office. When you build relationships, you are establishing trust. When you socialize, avoid talking about your previous career and your past. Tales about your previous life communicate all the wrong messages. They only indicate that you are still thinking about your past and they make you seem self-important. Briefing the President or the Secretary of Defense is not something that most civilians ever expect or want to do. Save the memory for friends and family and not at work.

Be unpretentious. You may think you already are, but become really unpretentious. Ask questions, seek coaching. Your colleagues can already tell you don't know much. Nodding gravely and pretending to understand the issue under discussion fools nobody. Instead study more and ask for assistance. People forgive a lot of someone making an honest effort. (Remember that if you were sponsoring a new civilian into your military unit that you would intuitively know the limits of the rookie's comprehension).

From Hero to Zero and Back!

When you see a member of your team routinely meeting with a peer or even your boss, your first response is likely to be annoyance. Instead accept it as just another thread of the spider web. Many of the relationships around you may be 10 to 20 years in the making. Focus on meaningful relationships as they are absolutely essential to your survival. Think of the beat of the tom-tom warning the tribe of news or danger.

> Begin by studying organizational history.

To be successful in a management position you must hear what the rest of the tribe does. If you are the lone member who hears nothing you are exposed in a way that you don't want to be. It's essential that you have a tenured member of the team interpret what others are hearing because you probably won't understand it. That will not happen unless you cultivate the relationships that will make that happen. You hear the CEO is unhappy. Why? What is everybody else going to do to address the issue? When does he expect the change to be implemented?

> Examine how your peers interact with one another and the boss when decisions are being made.

In your previous world you may have been the CEO. Now you probably aren't, the CEO seldom talks to you, so you go from being one the primary tribal elders to an aging team member who is out in the open when others are taking cover.

Good relationships lead to friendships over time. My experience in my first job was one of loneliness. I was too focused on "success," did not understand how to establish relationships in my new company and consequently found few genuine friendships. As a Veteran, I suggest that nothing is more important to us than the cherished camaraderie of our military experience. You may not be able to replicate this in your new life, but you can certainly try, and the rewards can be rich in many ways.

Decision-Making

As an executive or manager nothing could be more important than understanding how decisions are made in your company and who makes them.

I have touched on some obvious differences between your previous experience and the corporate world, including corporate proclivity to achieve consensus. The "spider's web" model diffuses organizational boundaries and challenges your ability to focus. I cautioned you to be respectful of the different speeds at which bureaucracies operate. Not everyone intends to make quick decisions. Some teams even resist the perceived need for major decisions, believing that minor adjustments are best.

What else should you know? Begin by studying organizational history. Is the company a confederation of previously independent entities? What form of Merger and Acquisition (M&A) strategy brought them together? Which part of the business generates revenue and profitability? Which areas(s) of the business is a cost center? These factors can assist you in determining where organizational decision-making is done.

You will also need to determine the framework for decision-making. Most companies use some version of strategic planning for the "out years", then transition to "budget year planning" the same as the DoD.

> Develop the habit of having a friend or mentor tell you afterwards "what really went on."

Take time to learn the inputs and desired outputs. Then learn how your team frames major choices and where the real work is done to develop an issue for decision. Learn where and when the boss speaks or provides intent. Framing of recommended courses of action is probably not done in the open. You may find out that unusual patterns like "end runs" by a favorite or favored few dominate the process. Study how much thought is given to "enterprise" level thinking versus speaking only for your own role.

Examine how your peers interact with one another and the boss when decisions are being made. This is another situation where the subtlety of civilian communications requires careful study. Many of us were accustomed to frank, open debate prior to decision. In your new world, pre-decisional discussion may be more muted and subtle. Your ability to speak may be limited by your position. On your new team votes may also be disproportionately given to "Profit and Loss" leaders vs "Staff." Learn your place by dipping your toes carefully in the water with brief, thought out remarks instead of strident advocacy. Develop the habit of having a friend or mentor tell you afterwards "what really went on" and how you were perceived during the meeting to sharpen your awareness of process and personalities.

Building Your Tool Kit

The goal of this section is to provide you the "tools" to operate successfully in the corporate world.

Mentorship

Your need for good mentors established in your military career increases the further you go into becoming a member of the commercial world. You need mentors who share two goals with you.
- An honest relationship.
- A smooth and successful transition from military to private business.

Ideally, at least one of your mentors should work in the same company as you and can see how you're doing. As a condition of accepting the job offer, I suggest that you request and receive a mentor designated by your boss. That person needs to be a willing sponsor and be a wise and perceptive individual. Your mentor (or hopefully mentors) should provide a combination of on the spot observations (as feasible) and schedule regular meetings to provide constructive feedback from a variety of sources. You should seek both technical and cultural input designed to make you more effective. Develop a thick skin and take specific steps to fix issues brought to you. I learned a saying early on – "feedback is the greatest gift" – and have lived by it.

> As a condition of accepting the job offer, I suggest that you request and receive a mentor designated by your boss.

Humility

Just about everybody thinks they are humble. In the transition you will learn whether you really are! Start by stripping away any memories of who you once were. Don't bring in your "I love me" photos and testimonials from your last life for the wall of your office. Make it clear that your military title does not belong on your business card (unless you have a representational role). Stop anybody when they try to use your former military rank as a form of address. Introduce yourself by your first name. The commercial workplace – interactions with superiors, subordinates and peers – can "appear" to be very casual. Get used to the new norm. When you speak don't be surprised if nobody listens. Recognize that you are now probably in a multi-generational work environment. Different generations process information differently. Questions and challenges to your thinking and guidance will be much more direct and may seem disrespectful. Don't fall back on your military mindset. Your job now is to listen and absorb what you are being told. If you are truly flexible you can probably adapt or adopt the suggestions while continuing to pursue your idea. But that may not be wise. A better approach may be to thank your teammates and pull your idea back for refinement.

> Develop a thick skin and take specific steps to fix issues...

> Don't bring in your "I love me" photos and testimonials from your last life for the wall of your office.

The "old days" where your position, power and seniority could compel obedience are gone. You will quickly squander your credibility if you invest it in defending a poorly received idea. Then, let's say that in response to your "defeat", you hastily set up a meeting to fix the identified issues – very risky. Do not assume that the challenges conveyed to you were personal. It is entirely possible that you do not fully understand the concerns expressed. Also, people are busy and may not be inclined to participate with you on short notice. If they do agree to meet, they may have no authority to authorize a new approach. You could have anticipated all of this had you had consulted your mentors. So, slow down, take a breath, do your research, and gain the counsel of your colleagues before you venture out to re-launch an idea discarded once already.

From Hero to Zero and Back!　　　　　　　　　　　　　　　　43

There is also the "24-hour rule" to be considered. When possible, after a defeat, wait 24 hours before acting. When you head home from work after your first month you should have a pretty good idea about how far you have "fallen" in your new life. By then, you should realize that your weak technical background and uncertain skills at personal relationships put you at risk. To survive these risks, exercise caution, work at new relationships, study hard and practice genuine humility – not false modesty. Work on these issues the way you would prepare for the actual job itself.

> Recognize that you are now probably in a multi-generational work environment.

Communication and Observation

If you ask a military leader how to communicate, you can be sure he/she will tell you how to speak. In the real world, communication is a two-way street and your most underdeveloped skills are listening and observing.

There is a reason that business schools advocate a "mindful" approach to personal interactions and communications. "Mindful" in this context means self-aware, under control, and observant. As a new member of a corporate management team, resist the urge to hit a home run in your first turn at bat. Be "mindful" of your lack of standing in the organization. Think of yourself as a benchwarmer recently called up from the minors in time for the World Series. Just sit in the dugout and take it all in – be thrilled you are part of the team. Your task is to observe, ask questions and be ready when you are called to pinch hit. Sharpen your observational skills and miss nothing. Watch who schedules meetings, how the agenda is set, how ideas are informally brought up for consideration.

> In the real world, communication is a two-way street and your most underdeveloped skills are listening and observing.

Be a part of the process wherever you can be. Don't try to take over. Initially your victory is just being invited to the party. Over time, progress can be

> As a new member of a corporate management team, resist the urge to hit a home run in your first turn at bat.

measured by being asked for your thoughts and then – finally – being relied on. This could take a year or longer. Be patient.

Loyalty

As Veterans we think we have a monopoly on loyalty. You will find loyalty in abundance in the commercial world; it's just framed differently. Learn to cherish it! First is brand loyalty. Companies work incredibly hard to define their brand and believe in it passionately. Study "the brand" in all its dimensions. Brand defines the way a company communicates both internally and externally. Fulfilling brand definition is a goal of corporate strategy so the company invests heavily in doing this. The brand exists to meet customer needs. Study the company's customers with similar intensity. Successful companies know their customer base intimately and strive to satisfy it with their products in all ways possible. They cherish their customers and work to expand both the number of customers and the depth of their relationship with them. Your understanding of this is vital to your success.

> Far too many former high ranking military officers have behaved poorly – at times criminally – in the workplace…

Morals and Conduct

The steady stream of news documenting moral failures within the military has guaranteed that this would be an issue in the private sector. Far too many former high ranking military officers have behaved poorly – at times criminally - in the workplace, exhibiting bad language, alcoholism, sexual promiscuity and sexual harassment. It is almost as if some former Soldiers believe that if the Uniform Code of Military Justice no longer applies, they are free to do as they please. They will learn – often the hard way – that commercial businesses have requirements every bit as strict as those in the Military.

> Begin by listening and not transmitting.

Modern companies perform serious pre-hiring background checks maintain investigative functions in their HR offices, monitor electronic and social media, and unlike the Military, can move with lightning speed to make changes. If you stumble be prepared to be shown the door with few chances to appeal.

Performance Assessment

Despite stories in trade publications about companies abandoning annual performance reviews, expect to find one in place where you wind up working. Typically, performance objectives are related to your role in executing corporate strategy. When you study the company be very diligent in learning learn how things are done:
- How broadly are goals set?
- Do the goals set for you link directly to those of your bosses?
- What defines success?
- What are your responsibilities to the people who report to you?
- What performance counselling should you receive through a year?

Be careful to set aside your previous definitions of "what is right" when issues of performance and potential come up. In the Army, we place great importance on the "senior rater's" role, believing that your bosses' boss has a superior perspective from which to pass judgement as well as an obligation to serve as a mentor.

When I tried to bring my sense of what a "senior rater" could contribute to the organization, resistance was substantial. My colleagues believed that this was the rater's job and additional help was neither needed nor welcomed. This is another example that your job upon arrival is to fit in with the established culture and not to disrupt it with ideas carried over from the military. As a new hire, you are probably ill-equipped to undertake such a change without good and ample reason – or a specific request – to do so.

Taking Charge

This one is simple. DO NOT TAKE CHARGE!

As military leaders many of us have been schooled to "seize the guidon" with enthusiasm. We are taught that our team's chances of responding to us positively decrease unless we act dramatically from the start. This generates an inevitable push to lead by making changes upon arrival. Frequently the arrival of a new leader signals new operational requirements. This makes the new leader's job of becoming in tune with his/her unit easier.

In the military tasks like "prepare to deploy to Europe for a year" have a way of captivating Soldiers while emphasizing key skills to be burnished or implemented. Consequently, we have learned how to come in with a thought-out message, capture attention, and ensure that everybody is intent on implementing that message. As you have guessed, it probably won't work now. Your skill set in this new commercial setting is too weak. Instead of standing in front of "your troops", I advocate the reverse approach. Begin by listening and not transmitting. Resist the urge to speak out and speak up. Recognize your considerable technical shortcomings. Invest your time in "spending a day" with various members of your team. Learn their skills. Begin to appreciate the depth of their professionalism. Break down their stereotypes of you. Ask your leaders to explain their jobs in detail. Solicit study material from them. Come back to them with questions after you have read their stuff. Convince them that you are deadly serious about learning their technical skills. Seek their advice about what you should be doing; learn how you can help them. Develop and execute a plan to meet and learn about your peers across your company or division. Make the pace slow enough so that you can absorb what you hear. Set priorities about who you meet and in what order. (I found that the quick effort to meet everybody in 10 days resulted in mental overload and limited actual retention). Recognize that each meeting should be preceded by study on your part. Read bios, job descriptions, rating schemes so you are at prepared to engage in a thoughtful, personal, and professional way.

Over time, try out ideas for change or improvement. Give credit to others for the ideas but only if warranted (no genuine person wants credit for something they did not earn). Measure success not by the volume of new ideas you bring in, but by their acceptance rate. As you can see from this approach, you are slowly building momentum and confidence. Any mistakes you make will be relatively unimportant and not long remembered. As you progress take broader and more sophisticated ideas and socialize them for implementation. Don't worry if at the end of your first year your list of significant accomplishments is limited. The important result is that you are still there and developing a reputation as a steady, reliable teammate who does his homework and is an increasingly accepted part of the company.

Strengthening Your Business Skills

Reporting

We are accustomed to monthly readiness reporting. Your new experience with monthly reporting will be very different. In the military our focus was on the adequacy of our resources followed by performance. Before we commented on the number of crews that qualified at a unit performance evaluation we first mentioned the inadequacy of leaders to fill slots, and the need for additional training time and resources.

Results were often second to identifying critical shortfalls that impinged on our ability to fulfill the mission. It's the opposite in the business world as reporting in this environment serves an entirely different purpose. Their meetings are all about performance and accountability focused on progress in executing the business plan. Results for publicly traded companies are released on a quarterly basis. Success or failure in meeting targets is measured monthly in detailed reports based on revenue and profit. And it's all based on the fundamentals of accounting.

> Be prepared to be a part of a continually evolving organization.

Some of the best advice I received (but regrettably never took) was to sign up for an accounting course to become professionally qualified in this basic skill. If you lack the time or ability for formal education, study hard with your mentor. Learn what your contribution to your businesses report is supposed to be and continue to grow until you understand the entire process. Keep and refer to a standard accounting text.

Understand that part of an executive's skill set is making or recommending adjustments to improve performance. Watch the process, learn who does what and who does it best. Figure out how to contribute. The likelihood that you are initially ready to play a strong role in this process is low. But fundamentals such as increasing sales and cutting costs should become quickly obvious.

Right Sizing

In the military we come from organizations designed by their respective Service (Army, Navy) to be correctly resourced for a specific application of military capability. A combat unit can execute attacks and defenses addressing a hypothetical enemy force. Over time they are adjusted in size or weapons or equipment to meet a unique operational requirement, but the blueprint remains relatively constant. The opposite is true in the commercial world. Be prepared to be a part of a continually evolving organization. The needs of the business dictate what it will be. A new marketing strategy exploiting a new customer relationship will probably result in corporate reorganization. Similarly, development of a major new product will probably generate a reconfiguration of assets to ensure it is fully supported. Levels or layers of organization change as the scope of the business evolves. New leaders bring new philosophies and frequently are accompanied by marked changes in structure. Quickly learn your position in the company. Be flexible if who you work for and how you are measured changes.

If you and your organization within the company are listed as "overhead" it means you are a "cost". Study how you contribute to the success of the larger team and be ready to be a thoughtful advocate for that value. Conversely, if the business is not achieving the plan in question, be prepared to recommend a more thoughtful one to reduce cost in your organization either by eliminating unnecessary functions or achieving greater efficiency to achieve desired results. Very often the term of reference is a Full Time Equivalent (FTE) meaning an employee. Every business measures the cost of their FTEs. Learn how your business measures FTE cost along with what your cost is to them.

> Your challenge is to learn that tipping point and live close to it.

When times are good, the focus will be to keep overhead constant to maximize profit. When times are bad, achieving reductions in overhead is the quickest way to rescue bad performance. Your ability to be a thoughtful part of assessing needed adjustments will be essential to your good standing.

Another framework to understand is organizational layering. In the military we have time honored layers from high command to the Soldier, Sailor, Airman, Marine or Coast Guardsman. In the business world there is nothing sacrosanct about organizational hierarchy. Flat organizations are desired wherever possible. As a result, you need to challenge layering of your organization. A business may have four levels of vice presidents (Assistant Vice President, Vice President, Senior Vice President, and Executive Vice President). Learn the expected level of responsibility for each. As you become accountable for your organization focus on understanding how each level contributes (or does not) to achieving the mission. Corporations strive to run "lean" and "flat". Your flexibility in understanding where your team stands in its resourcing level will be very useful to the larger organization. Wherever you reduce organization structure you cut cost and and improve performance at least to a point. (Use caution when recommending these cuts and carefully navigate the political landscape with acute awareness.) While the company may benefit from certain cuts, individuals – your colleagues – may not. Your challenge is to learn that tipping point and live close to it.

Crisis Management

As Veterans we often assume that we know how to deal with organizational crises. In the military we quickly learn how to activate a Crisis Action Team (CAT) to address the latest emergency. Again, I found that my Army instincts were not useful. I learned that responsibility for addressing the problem probably stays with the proponent for the issue in question. In contrast, Veterans are accustomed for the head of "Operations" to assume overall responsibility for coordinating the company's response.

In the private sector, if it's a public relations issue, the PR head will lead the effort. If it's a manufacturing issue, then the head of manufacturing is responsible. Others will be involved only on an "as needed" basis. Be careful before you provide your solution to "help".

Customer Focus

In the Military we may think we have "customer focus," yet it's rarely more than a slogan. In your new role you will quickly learn that successful businesses have extraordinarily deep relationships with their customers. Listen carefully to those in your company whose job it is to study the customer. Their insights are invaluable to guiding strategic development and initiatives. Where possible, interact with customers. Think of your relationship with the customer as a partnership. That is good business strategy.

Governance

Commercial companies are all founded on basic documents that establish the organization as a legal entity. Study how your company was founded and what its regulations are. Embedded in this are specific roles for groups or bodies that are a part of the company. Of importance are the roles of the Board of Directors, Chairman and CEO. If you are in senior management, how you relate to these people is vital to your success.

Chairmen can either be "executive" or "non-executive". You need to know the difference. The CEO can also be the chairman, though this is rare. When and how the Board meets and how their agenda is set for each meeting is vital to your planning. Normally the company's general counsel is the Board secretary and can help you get acquainted with the board. As each company is unique, you need to pick up the unique traditions regarding how they function and where you fit. If you are a senior officer in a company, your appearances in front of the Board is a key opportunity for you to shine.

Experiencing Failure and Recovery

Immediate Actions

What if – despite hard work to learn the ropes in your new world – you stumble and fail?

That can occur in two ways – your decision or theirs. You may be able to leave on your own terms in your own time. Assuming you are a military retiree you should have some income and thus some flexibility. If you have other job opportunities, the decision is that much easier. Still, be very careful regarding obligations to your current firm. If you are considering joining a competitor you may be either prohibited by a non-compete clause in your contract or be liable to legal action from the company you are leaving. Be aware of any commitments you made to your employer as a part of their investment in you.

Let's imagine that what happened to me happens to you. You walk in to work one day and are told that you no longer have a job, and everything changes. In most circumstances, you will be escorted off the premises immediately after notification. The company will pack and ship your personal items to you. They will lock you out of your company email and you will be asked to turn over your company issued communication devices. Therefore, whether you think you are on thin ice with the company or not, keep your personal data separate from your company data. Don't store personal documents at work. Maintain your own cell phone and email account.

> Let's imagine that what happened to me happens to you. You walk in to work one day and are told that you no longer have a job, and everything changes.

The company HR team will

notify employees that you have chosen to depart to "pursue other opportunities". You will be given some form of a severance offer which – as a matter of law – you cannot sign for several days. My suggestion is that when you are let go do not tell anyone what happened except your family. Decide whether you want to retain an attorney. Take your time, cool off.

Form a support group. We know from our military days that support groups are invaluable in times of crisis. Think carefully as you decide with whom you will share. You need some sympathy, but you also need advice to deal with complexities the business world understands but you don't.

After I was fired, my wife was key to shaping my daily attitude. My brother-in-law was an essential member of my support team, not just as a member of the family, but because as a senior corporate executive, he helped me understand what I could not. My employment attorney became a key friend as well as legal counsel.

Acceptance

Respond to your dismissal with a new perspective. In the commercial world management and executives are let go all the time. When it happened to me, I thought that it was the end of my professional life, comparable to the civilian equivalent of being relieved of command or conviction at a court martial. Since then, I have learned that many CEOs and other senior executives were fired at some point and rebounded to great success.

This is not the end of the world. The key to your future success will be how you manage the days and weeks after you have been let go. If there is anger, control it and realize that your future will be influenced by how you ended your relationship and what you decide to do next. Consider hiring legal counsel. A lawyer will help you understand your legal recourse (if there is any) and what it may cost. The terms of my proposed severance were very encumbering. By accepting their exit offer, I would have foreclosed important options for future career opportunities. I decided not to accept the severance offer and cash settlement and simply moved on instead. And be aware that retaining a lawyer and telling your former employer you have done so are two different things.

Once your former employer knows you have retained a lawyer they will probably request that all communications be from your lawyer to theirs. And that can become very expensive very quickly. Just because

From Hero to Zero and Back!

you hire an attorney does not mean you must announce it. When my lawyer and I studied my terms of employment, I learned that I had signed an agreement to binding arbitration. This meant that getting my case heard in court would be difficult. Be aware that large enterprises have existing relationships with many large law firms and thus they will be unable to represent you. That may limit your options, at first, in securing the counsel you want. Seek out smaller firms that are less likely to be working for your former company. When you meet with your lawyer be prepared to provide him/her with all your employee records. (Retain copies away from work). The first job of your attorney is to say whether you have legal grounds to contest your firing.

> In the commercial world management and executives are let go all the time.

A responsible lawyer will not only discuss potential grounds for action, but the probability of success as well as the overall process, time, and expense. With that information you will be able to make good decisions.

> Be aware that large enterprises have existing relationships with many large law firms and thus they will be unable to represent you.

Fighting Back

Minimize general discussion regarding the nature of your departure from your last employer. Keep the details to yourself! To all but your close friends and family say nothing. Develop some believable version of "I decided to leave to pursue other opportunities."

Although legally free to do so, your former employer will most likely not comment on what happened and only confirm that you were once an employee. Don't forget that they are legally free to talk about your departure. So, consider whether you are being asked to sign an agreement that would prohibit you from discussing your experiences there, leaving only one side of the story to be told.

At some point you will have to decide what you want to do next. You may want to go in an entirely new direction or not want employment at all. Wait until you are less emotional about getting fired to seriously think about it. If you are interested in jumping back

> Develop some believable version of "I decided to leave to pursue other opportunities."

into the game, say so! Develop a generally accurate (but not dishonest) explanation of your previous situation that protects your good name.

Figure out who the best references from your last job might be and take them into your confidence. Be sure they know how you are describing the nature of your departure. Be forewarned as prospective employers will contact them and attempt to gain insights about why you left. Know that a substantial number of former military leaders fail in their first civilian employment. This experience is common place in the commercial world.

> Know that a substantial number of former military leaders fail in their first civilian employment.

For most of us, the central issue leading to our departure was a poor "job fit". This was certainly true for me! I was trying to be something I really was not and felt like I was living in a glass cage. Over time both employer and employee mutually realize that your skills are not aligned with the task and your workstyle is not compatible with the culture. When that happens, it is only a matter of time until the relationship ends.

Now I know the joy of working alongside a lean management team devoted to supporting the production workers at our assembly plant. Communications are clear and to the point. Strategic discussions involve everybody because we all are intimately involved in the outcomes. People look out for each other. They have a heartfelt authenticity that I find welcoming and fulfilling. In my heart this team has replaced the Soldiers that I knew and loved. I am proud of what they do and how they do it – with so many working hard on their feet all day while taking enormous pride in our product. I am humbled that my fellow employees hold me and the rest of the team accountable to their high standards.

In my second turn in the corporate world I have been much less focused on the trappings of "management" and much more focused on being part of a proud and caring team that closely replicates my pride in the Army. My self-assessment about what I did wrong in my

> My self-assessment about what I did wrong in my first job guided my approach in my second one.

first job guided my approach in my second one. Learning from my past I took the time to learn the business, devoted time to cultivating relationships with all levels of the organization, studied our customer and business partners before implementing any far-reaching modifications. Over time we have reduced the layers in the organization, promoted team focused leaders, changed products, renovated our marketing plan and improved business procedures. But this was a gradual process of small changes accompanied by continual communication and feedback to ensure we kept the team together. I had learned that making changes in corporate environments cannot be done as if it was a brief battle, but rather as a long campaign taking years to achieve.

Health

In the Army, a day spent away from work was to be avoided if possible. Over my years of Service, I probably took less than five days off for health reasons. This lifestyle was enabled by a medical system developed for senior leaders that resembled a NASCAR pit team. Their job was to slosh some fuel into us, change worn tires and push us back out on the track. I aided and abetted that approach by minimizing whatever health issues I encountered out of concern that it would limit my utility to the Army.

Making it more dangerous was the awareness that our most admired senior leaders functioned with little or no sleep. Visiting Iraq during the height of our operations in Iraq I remember seeing the commanding general's helicopter lift off every day at 5:30 AM having already responded to all overnight emails. In the Pentagon, a similar ethic prevailed. I remember getting a call at 5:45 AM from my boss two levels above me. He was following up on an action I'd sent him just before midnight.

> And yet, even "Ironmen" wake up one day and can't take the field due to health.

And yet, even "Ironmen" wake up one day and can't take the field due to health. My challenges began shortly after I retired and required time and attention to fix. I attribute much of this to my previous life in the military and only discuss it to make others aware that while we may not be chronologically old, we have a lot of miles on us! Making time for self and seeking thorough, long-delayed medical care should be a part of your new life from the start. I believe that the health issues I experienced played a part in issues I have had as a civilian trying to concentrate and learn new environments. I did not realize that the symptoms I was experiencing – such as difficulty in staying awake – were treatable and would have been a direct impact in doing my civilian job.

Concluding Thoughts

Envisioning Success

Take on this new phase in your life with enthusiasm and honesty. You should be searching for self-fulfillment as much as income. Your search for employment should be governed by your soul if you hope to replace the void in your spirit that the military occupied. If it does not feel right don't do it! Money alone is not enough. Think of the future as an entirely new adventure. Understand that as a Veteran you bring great strengths to your new workplace.

Let's enumerate those strengths so you remember them. You are:
- Smart, adaptive and resilient
- Comfortable dealing with disorganization and complexity
- Able to assess risk and deal with it
- Loyal and group focused
- Creative, and poised
- Multi-cultural
- Honest and hard-working
- Physically fit

To hire someone with the above attributes, prospective employers are willing to commit to re-training and developing you in their profession. In almost all cases they understand that you will be a "work in progress" for many months. You must show progress and hard work to reward that investment. This is your next deployment to a strange new land! As best as you are able, cut the strings to your old persona and develop new capabilities to enable your new mission.

Just as you are conscious of your strengths as a former Servicemember, also be aware of your limitations. In the world that you are joining people routinely work very hard. Your new associates lack much of the security you are used to. They are ready to adapt quickly and have mastered their profession. While you have well-honed qualities of devotion to duty, pride and loyalty, so do they. Become proud to be a new kind of professional. Embrace what makes them good at what they do. Celebrate success in their image and do not cling to the mentality that your real allegiance remains to the uniform. Once you settle in to your new identity, develop a personal vision of success and goals. Your second career may be much less illustrious than your previous one, but it can still be extremely fulfilling. At this stage of my life, success is simply keeping our small company going. That modest goal demands all the skills that I have developed over 43 years of working and learning.

> Your second career may be much less illustrious than your previous one, but it can still be extremely fulfilling.

Second Thoughts

The experience of becoming a civilian is strange and new. Let me give you an example of a question that came as a shock to me early in my new life. I had been at work about two months when out of the blue an old friend called me and asked if I wanted to be considered for an opportunity to lead a military college. In my heart I immediately said, YES! It had been a long-time dream about which I had done nothing. Yet, I decided as a matter of loyalty to stay where I was. In retrospect, I think I made the wrong choice.

> …if you have the chance to live the dream of a lifetime, go after it.

As a civilian you don't swear an oath to your new institution. Unless you have an employment contract (and most do not), you are an employee "at will". They will let you go when it suits them. I now believe that you should make such a choice based only on the latest opportunity and the dictates of your heart. Be prepared to pay back any signing bonus or transition expense incurred by your employer. As a retiree the number of years remaining for new opportunities is limited. I am not recommending whimsical job hopping but suggest you think freely. If in your new job you have been warmly welcomed and are successfully contributing, the last thing you should do is to leave. On the other hand, if you have the chance to live the dream of a lifetime, go after it. How often do people change jobs? It might be more often than you think. The era of being employed by one company for life is long over. Workers now migrate from job to job over their career in search of greater fulfillment and compensation. Employers discharge employees more readily than in the past. Great opportunities will probably not come back. Take them when offered.

Helping a Transitioning Veteran

This guide has been devoted to the transitioning military leader to provide him or her the tools to make better decisions in post-military life.

If you are an employer and want to help, you have enormous potential to make your firm "military friendly." You can shape your work environment to provide structure, culture, mentorship, and evaluation that will facilitate the Veteran's transition. After working with other transitioning Veterans as an employer my sense is that a "tough love" approach works best. In this context "tough" means candid and frank. Military leaders are used to that.

The After-Action Review (AAR) process the military uses to assess a just-completed event focuses on the decision-making and performance of leaders. In those sessions, leaders face scrutiny and hard questions in the presence of their subordinates and superiors. A former military member operating in a new and complex bureaucracy benefits from a well-defined work environment with clear expectations. Use that history to provide feedback that you would not normally give an employee who has never served our country.

> Your new employee will need a good diagnosis of skill deficiencies and a plan to fix them before they become fatal.

Put yourself in his/her position as you develop his role. Everything is new and your Veteran – having no relevant experience to draw on – needs help with structure. He or she needs a strong mentor, ideally one involved in creating the job opportunity. The mentor should be committed to the Veteran's success. Your new employee will need a good diagnosis of skill deficiencies and a plan to fix them before they become fatal. Develop and monitor the Veteran's training. Give him/her the opportunity to know and learn about the team. Other members of the team – including peers and direct reports – need to feel a responsibility for assisting their new teammate.

Be careful about placing too much responsibility on him/her before they are ready. Instead, consider progressively increasing the level of responsibility and expectations. Minimize the Veteran's expectations that instant performance is expected. Include him/her in the "behind the scenes" activity that sets up major meetings and processes. Realize that a Veteran cherishes being a part of the team and, when excluded, struggles. We all have an intense need to contribute and this is especially true of the Veteran finding their way in the civilian world.

Remember that new starts in life are always tough. They are hard in the military and they are also hard in business. As Veterans, history is a good place to put our journey in perspective. Our story began with Lawrence of Arabia encouraging study and genuine intellectual curiosity in examining a different form of warfare. In that spirit, look to the past for a seminal account of "America's First Battles." The book examines the first battles of America's wars, battles that often ended in defeat. Whether the battle was Kasserine Pass in World War II, or the Battle of Osan in the Korean War, we have too often begun a new campaign with tactical failure.

> As you deploy for the "first battle" of your civilian career, examine your skill set to make sure it's relevant and effective on your new battlefield.

The flaw was trying to fight the first battle of a new war with the techniques and weaponry of the previous one. As you deploy for the "first battle" of your civilian career, examine your skill set to make sure it's relevant and effective on your new battlefield. Armed with careful study and self-reflection your strengths as a Veteran will rise to facilitate your success in your next campaign!

For those who read this guide from outside the culture of the military keep the faith! Hire Veterans! The same qualities of character that distinguish Servicemembers in uniform can be yours. Imagine seeing the Veteran you hire demonstrate resilience in the face of setbacks, accepting cultural diversity as natural, being undeterred by chaos and complexity, and inspiring positive results from others.

Consider the value in extending many of the same opportunities you might extend to Veterans to other new employees. Imagine what your new human capital might deliver if every new arrival had a sponsor, or someone besides Human Resources to facilitate a transition?

My feelings about a career after the military are personal. As with most human experience, my emotions combine joy and satisfaction with heartache and pain. I am personally committed to sharing what I learned to help others. Most Veterans are more vulnerable than we initially assume and need more assistance than we would guess. But, it is a journey worth making when compared to the alternative, which is to live in a military cocoon for the rest of our days. As Veterans we have an obligation to "pass it forward". We can do so by sharing lessons from our civilian experiences to help others who follow us make their new lives rewarding and meaningful.

Appendices

a. Career Planning Checklists
b. Your Resume
c. Tips for Success
d. Glossary

a.
Career Planning Checklists

This section provides the checklists for major developments – a quick reference source preparing for the activities described. They appear along with amplification and further description.

Self-Assessment
Take the time to do an honest self-examination as you start your transition planning.
- How hard do I want to work?
- Do I want to retain my military identity or start over outside of the DoD environment?
- Are my values in line with pursuing charity, volunteer work, or commercial success?
- Do I want to work independently or as a member of a team?
- Where do I want to live?
- What is important to my family?
- How important is additional income?
- What are my fellow military retirees in the civilian world doing and how are they enjoying it?

What you want to learn from a job description.
- How is the job defined?
- Where is the job?
- What qualifications do they establish?
- Who will you work for?

- Is the job a developmental opportunity?
- How does the firm describe itself and their hiring goals?

Your initial information requirements when meeting a recruiter.
- What is the hiring process?
- What is the job – not just as described in the posting but in reality?
- What can the recruiter tell you about "the real intent" of his client not evident in writing?
- When do they want to make their selection?
- What are the most important attributes they are looking for?
- Where is the job located?
- Who will you report to?
- Are there any significant lifestyle issues you should know about up front, such as continuous travel?

Take notes following an interview, person by person.
- What did they ask?
- How did you grade yourself?
- Where did you shine?
- Where were you weak?

Derived Knowledge

Learn these points to shape your thinking about job fit.
- Is the opportunity new to the organization?
- If not new, what happened to the previous holder of your new position?
- Why the previous job holder leave?
- Do you have a clear understanding of who you are working for and what requirements await?
- Are your new peers and direct reports ready for you to assume your role?
- Do you have a sponsor?
- Is that person responsible for making you successful?
- What technical and cultural training will you receive?
- What reputation does your new employer have on social media?

From Hero to Zero and Back! 65

- What do Veteran's groups think about the company?

Compensation and Benefits
- Ask the hiring authority to explain the intellectual basis for their salary proposal:
- How is your job being categorized and why? (Jobs are developed for a specific level based on programmatic and/or supervisory responsibility, and seniority.)
- Are they using a local or national pay salary comparability scheme? (Firms set most compensation packages against a standard.)
- At what level of peers' compensation are they benchmarking their salaries at? (For example, some leading national firms will benchmark at 90% meaning that they intend for your pay to be equal to or better than 90% of the population. Others set more modest goals — for example at 50%.)
- Beyond base pay, you will want to know the following in detail:
    o How your bonus eligibility is determined. Ask the HR team to show you with the most recent company performance data how your bonus would translate to income.
    o How much is in stock and how much is in cash?
    o Whether the company allows you to defer your bonus so you do not create a higher tax burden.
    o Will your bonus "vest"? (Become yours) even if you terminate your employment or are terminated?
    o When can you retire from the company?
    o What the company's 401K plan and how the company "matches" employee contributions?

Performance Assessment
As a part of your company research you should be diligent in learning how they assess performance.
- How broadly are goals set?

- Do they link directly to your bosses?
- What defines success?
- What are your responsibilities for your direct reports?
- What counselling is required over the year?

Mentorship
You need mentors who are committed to your success.
- The mentor must be totally honest.
- The mentor should be in, or have been in, a position to guide and assist you in making the transition.
- The mentor should be well connected in your firm so the he/she is providing you wise counsel drawn from the spectrum of people you interact with.
- He/she must make time for you, both for scheduled meetings and for impromptu conversations.

Your Strengths as a Transitioning Veteran
Use them to help you tell your personal story as they relate to you.
- Smart and adaptive
- Resilient
- Comfortable dealing with chaos and complexity
- Able to assess and deal with risk
- Loyal and affiliative
- Creative and positive
- Multi-cultural
- Sociable
- Poised
- Honest
- Hard-working

b
Your Resume

In the second chapter "Decision Point" I provided some thoughts on how to set up your resume and recommended you consult a guide book on the topic.

Recently, I was advising a new retiree concerned that he was getting "no bites" in his job search. I asked to see his resume and told him that I was not surprised. It was more disappointing to learn that he had consulted with a professional service and that organization had "remade" his resume in their image of success.

After we had several conversations he developed a resume he felt comfortable with (unlike his earlier version). He quickly received inquiries and was quickly employed. More importantly, he told me that his interviews were much stronger because the process he used to build his resume enabled him to describe his qualifications when he was interviewed.

My thoughts on how to build your resume have little to do with how it looks and everything to do with what you think about yourself and what you want to accomplish with it. So, throw the sample of your friend's resume away and start fresh focused only on telling your story. Format comes easily after you have built your career story and focused on your employment goals. Build a resume that combines elements of a chronological structure with what is termed a "functional" description of your career as you will discuss it when you interview.

Include your spouse or significant other in the process – you need somebody who refuses to indulge in our proclivity for acronyms and "military speak" over conversational English.

The process below will help to organize your thoughts in reverse order from how they will appear on your resume. Build from that base and then move up so the words at the top of your resume are your own thoughts about how you want to summarize yourself at an interview. A clear and engaging resume is your best bet for a company to schedule you for an interview. In many cases, this will be the story that gets you in the door.

Chronological Summary

Go back ten years and in reverse order (the most recent at the top) provide a job description that begins with your job title followed in parentheses by what that job means in civilian terms. Include a short description of your responsibilities.

To those who dispute the use of "civilian terms," I offer the following: I have read several resumes that even I cannot understand. If they don't work for somebody who has served with and maintains close ties to the military then it is virtually impossible that anyone else will be able to fathom it. All it takes is one person who does not understand for you to lose a critical vote in the hiring process. For each step in writing your resume I will provide you an extract from mine to show you what it looks like. A sample job description from my resume follows:

- **DEPUTY COMMANDING GENERAL, MAJOR GENERAL, ARMY FORCES IN KUWAIT 2003 – 2004 (DEPUTY FOR LOGISTICS TO THE CEO)**
  LED PLANNING AND EXECUTION FOR LIFE SUPPORT OF ALL GROUND FORCES OPERATING IN IRAQ AND AFGHANISTAN, SUPERVISING 20,000 DEPLOYED MILITARY AND CIVILIAN PERSONNEL. PLANNED AND EXECUTED THE FIRST RELIEF IN PLACE OF FORCES IN IRAQ, MOVING 250,000 SOLDIERS AND MARINES AND THEIR EQUIPMENT IN AND OUT OF IRAQ. SUCCESSFULLY BUILT A NONSTANDARD ORGANIZATION OF 20,000 MILITARY AND CIVILIAN PERSONNEL TO MEET LOGISTICAL NEEDS OF OUR ARMY AND MARINE FORCES IN COMBAT.

Capability Development

As you write each job description think carefully about what you did in that job – it will be used for the next part of the process. From the description above I could derive you have a capacity for "logistics and supply chain" expertise as well as "high performance team leadership."

Jot those thoughts down as you work. Once you have finished your chronology of key jobs you should have a good feel for what capabilities you wish to talk about in your interviews as your <u>achievements.</u> Prioritize them. The key capabilities I chose (in addition to the ones cited) were: *Strategic Planning, Transformation, Business Partnerships, Communication, Budget Administration/DoD Acquisition and Organizational Development.*

After you have refined your "capabilities" illustrate how you have used them for success in one or more of your jobs as previously described. They are your "achievements." This is how I addressed my capability to enable and lead company organizational development in terms of achievements:

- ORGANIZATIONAL DEVELOPMENT
  REDUCED THE COMPANY'S STRUCTURE FROM **5 LAYERS TO 3. CUT OVERHEAD 25%.** REORGANIZED CORPORATE LEADERSHIP INTEGRATION AROUND **A THEME OF "COLLABORATION AND SHARING".** ALIGNED COMPANY MARKETING TO ADDRESS NEW CUSTOMERS. **REORGANIZED ASSEMBLY AND PRODUCTION OPERATIONS TO IMPROVE PERFORMANCE, ENHANCE ACCOUNTABILITY, AND IMPROVE QUALITY.** BROUGHT IT FUNCTION TO THE FOREFRONT OF COMPANY ATTENTION TO HARNESS NEEDED SYNERGIES FROM PROPER USE OF SAP. CREATED A **"TRUST BASED"** EMPLOYEE TRAINING PROGRAM TO BUILD A CULTURE OF INDIVIDUAL AND LEADER ACCOUNTABILITY AND SHARING.

Note the absence of technical vernacular, the simplicity of description. Once you have illustrated your achievements take them to a trusted confidant and with a straight face tell him/her how you are excelled in leading "Organizational Development." If you get a "go," you can be confident that you will be successful in using that description in your interview.

Executive Description

At the top of your resume characterize yourself as you want your potential employer to see you. For me, this was the hardest part of the process. We think of ourselves in the military as "jacks of all trades, and masters of anything." That does not sell well in the civilian world. The burden is on you to describe yourself in terms that will be useful to somebody who is hiring for a specific job.

As you review your draft resume, think through how some of your responsibilities compare with jobs and professions in the civilian sector. The experience(s) that makes you most employable may not be your last or the most senior job.

Several years ago, I pointed out to a retiring officer that his job as a garrison commander (which he held many years ago) was likely his most useful in finding a new career as a city manager, at which he remains happily employed.

For those who truly are generalists, we may have to adopt the self-description I used – "Executive Management" – followed by key terms that describe me as I want to be seen. To buttress that, I could point out that as a leader or member of a senior staff, I had very specific capabilities that appeared in the resume.

Executive Management
• Transformational Leadership • Strategic Planning & Execution • Business Reengineering

A visionary, creative, and decisive leader who inspires thoughtful solutions to achieve the organizational mission.

Results Oriented • Mentor and Coach
DOD Budget Expertise

Now, you have built your resume, so let's assemble your work for review:

Stephen M (Steve) Speakes
Email:
Cell:

Executive Management
• Transformational Leadership • Strategic Planning & Execution • Business Reengineering

Achievements
High Performance Team Leadership

PROFESSIONAL EXPERIENCE
- President and CEO of Kalmar RT Center, LLC, Cibolo, Texas • 2013 – Present

EDUCATION / PROFESSIONAL DEVELOPMENT

LANGUAGES (Optional)

COMMUNITY SERVICE (Optional)

If we have done this right your completed product is between a page-and-a-half to two pages long (but no more), and is useful to you. My test for my resume came on short notice when I was invited to a

From Hero to Zero and Back!

dinner with a prospective employer which became my interview. Before heading out, I jotted the capabilities from my resume on a 3x5 card and brought the card along. During the dinner I had it for reference in my pocket and made sure to address those points thoroughly during our conversation. (I got the job!)

I hope that taking the mythology out of the process and focusing on storytelling will help Veterans like us who have never developed a resume avoid traps that focus on format and complexity instead of simplicity and utility.

To conclude this section, here is a final suggestion. Tailor your resume to the actual job you are interviewing for. One job may demand project management experience. The next may prioritize your ability to operate in multiple cultures. Both elements are in your skill set, but may demand different billing as you prepare for a specific interview.

c
Tips for Success

Now that you are negotiating our "strange new world," you might appreciate some random lessons I acquired by my experience. Here are some highlights of less spoken about but true "rules" by which you will learn to live.

Interacting with DoD employees

As a former military senior leader, you may find that despite your strong desire to avoid falling back into the DoD orbit you must deal with DoD as a "contractor." If you are not a national figure like the Chief of Staff or the Chairman of the Joint Chiefs of Staff it's quite the experience! Civilian employees with whom I interacted as a contractor took pains to call me "Mr. Speakes". I found civilians almost always called me "Mister" or nothing at all. I have thought about why and have concluded that they have seen too many former senior leaders who still believe that their rank "matters" as they conduct business as civilians. From my perspective, being called "general" means about as much as calling a former diplomat "ambassador" or a former jurist "judge", but they apparently don't see it that way. To you it should be a nicety, but nothing more. The next bridge to cross is interacting with Soldiers still in service. Almost universally I find them professionally courteous, but cautious. They want to keep it professional – as they should. You need to do your part.

When I correspond with a DoD employee I almost always use rank or a formal salutation (Colonel or Mr./Ms.) to ensure that nobody mistakes my professional correspondence for anything other than that. When I see an old comrade, I allow about one minute for social niceties before moving on. If we still or did have a personal relationship, we don't purse it in the office. Be ready to deal with something you may have inflicted on others – however necessary - during your service that comes back to bite you.

You can also experience prolonged waits to be seen by your appointment or having it postponed at the last minute. You make an appointment, travel to see a military leader with whom you are familiar and are either not seen at all or made to wait for an uncomfortable stretch of time. This happens to people like you all the time so do not take it personally.

Also, be prepared to be met in circumstances that are not in keeping with your former status. My most humorous experience was when a former officer who was now a civilian employee put me in a chair in front of him in a crowded office. The chair was probably a deliberate choice by him as it was so low to the ground that my knees were up alongside my ears as he stared down at me from above. I knew he was trying to get my goat so I deliberately did not respond to his choice of seating. Afterward, I thanked him for knowing that I had back issues and needed just such a chair!

Corporate Correspondence

When you interact with your new corporate counterparts be thoughtful about your new environment. I have found civilians are more formal than those in the Service when writing an email, so use spell check. In the military, correspondence usually elicited a prompt response. We tend to think of our experience with tactical radio communications – if you did not hear an acknowledgement you were unsure that your message was received. Civilians may not routinely acknowledge your note (even if you asked a question or confirmation). The attitude in the private sector is much more trusting – you sent it to me, of course I read it, don't worry about it. Be aware of what time of day you are sending correspondence. If you are of the habit of dashing off emails before you go to sleep or when you wake up, be careful not to inflict that on your new counterparts without observing their communication patterns first. In the military we tend to admire the "always on duty" approach. In the commercial world it hints to being out of balance. Worse yet, you may be giving the impression that you may expect folks to be reading your notes before midnight or before breakfast. This same caution extends to weekend correspondence: check and see how others operate before communicating routine thoughts.

Finally, watch your address groups. When I wrote an email that inadvertently conveyed a misperception or violation of a cultural norm I found to my chagrin that it had been widely shared with others. Protect yourself by being selective about what you put in written correspondence and whom you send it to. Less of both is probably better, particularly when you are just starting.

DoD Ceremonies

As a retiree you will be on some protocol office's list of invitees. When you show up for the event, you will probably be early. The folks who will arrive ahead of time with you will probably also be retirees. So

From Hero to Zero and Back! 75

how does it go? You will be amazed.

Increasingly, I've come to believe that as we age we become what we really are. If you struggled with your weight while on active duty, you blossom in retirement. If you were lean and fit, you are likely to become lean and gaunt. Many of us develop medical issues shortly after retiring. As a group we age fast and I doubt that when lined up against actuarial tables we live as long as our civilian counterparts.

So, what do you do when you see your former colleagues? The ritual greeting is "Sam or Sally, you look GREAT!". And everybody will tell you that you look GREAT. When talk turns to life in retirement, there is another standard line, "It's WONDERFUL!"

When the active military and civilians arrive – folks whose lives are busier and more hectic than yours is now – expect them to be just in time. Exchanges with them will likely be brief before they dash back to work. They are busy and important and you are probably neither at this stage of the game. When the ceremony is over you will probably find yourself back again among your retired friends because everybody else has hurried back to work!

Your Health

We have drawn on our bodies to propel us through an exciting and demanding profession. Unfortunately, about the time we retire is the time for payback to begin. In the years prior to your transition take the time to address your health. Do not put off fixing things "until you retire." You would not do that to a car you owned and you should not do it to yourself.

Begin to document the things that need fixing and make a list of those you've been told "can't be fixed." In your dealings with the Veterans Administration post retirement, all your claims regarding disability must be documented. Enduring or chronic issues should not wait "until you have the time." The time is now.

As you make your choice about where you want to live in retirement think carefully about medical care availability. Continued reliance on Tricare and access to military facilities is not to be assumed as a retiree.

Fitness

When I retired I lost the primary rituals associated with my fitness regime. Gone was unit PT, the weigh in, the PT Test. In its place I had many good intentions which did not work out (because I wasn't working out!) I gained weight and was unhappy with myself. My first mistake was in believing that a home gym would be a success. It did not work. For me, a fitness routine had to be social. Not that I want to talk to others when I am exercising, I did want to be in a pleasant, uplifting environment where others were exercising around me. So, I joined a nice gym.

This helped, but still was not everything I needed. Things took off when my wife and I went to a fitness club and signed up for a coach and regular workout sessions. I found out that my knowledge of fitness from the military was not only dated but largely irrelevant to what a 60-year-old needed to be doing. Under my coach's guidance, I began a constantly varying routine that emphasized the kind of routine necessary for a middle-aged male. The new drill featured balance, agility, and core strength, not endless hours on a treadmill or bench presses. I believe that my time spent in fitness has been the best investment of my new life.

Social Presence

Do you have an active presence in social media? Do you know how to use it to assist your transition?

Everyone has heard that maintaining a presence is important, but we probably know little about how to do it. Here are a couple of quick thoughts.

First, this isn't about being on *Facebook*. Focus on establishing your presence on business social media. The preeminent means to do that currently is *Linked In*. Establishing a *Linked In* account requires time and energy, and is generally consistent with the other steps necessary to get you "transition ready", such as preparing your resume.

Much of your resume can be tailored to fit on a social media account. A *Linked In* account will help you get your feet wet with an incredibly powerful tool for cultural awareness and job finding. Becoming familiar with the many facets of *Linked In* requires time and practice. To become good at it, give yourself a progressive set of tasks. First, set up your account. Then invite somebody to your account that you want to be your *Linked In* "friend." Then, find a post you enjoy or support and "like" it as a form of endorsement.

Then, post something of your own. Study the jobs site. Understand how to know when somebody is "checking you out". Don't wait until you have retired and looking for work to get started like many of your retiring colleagues have done. It's almost humorous to see the new account appear with the "transitioning military professional" label. My response when I see the new account is disappointment that such a fundamental part of transition has been left until its needed.

c.
Glossary

Readers of this Guide will probably come from two very distinct communities. One will be former members of the Military. The other set will be life-long civilians who have had little interaction with Servicemembers. This section informally bridges the gap and facilitates understanding for both sets of readers.

For the Military Audience

"At Will" Employee: The term used to describe the status of most civilian employees. Most employees have no contract. They can be let go, or they can choose to depart with no contractual requirement.

Budget and Forecast: The two terms are used somewhat differently in various companies, and differently than in DoD. The term "budget" is customarily used in the commercial world to describe the current annual plan. Frequently it is treated as the company's "contract" with the Board and with Shareholders and serves as the basis for annual and quarterly evaluation of a company's performance. The term "forecast" usually refers to the continuous updating of the budget based on the latest business conditions and performance. It is usually updated monthly.

Direct Reports: It is the civilian term for "subordinates". Many corporations use matrix management for shared services such as human resources, finance, and legal. The people performing those functions will customarily not be direct reports of those business departments they support.

FTE: This acronym stands for "Full Time Equivalent". The commercial world treats the workforce as their most important and controllable expense. As a department leader a corporate executive is expected to know their organization's FTEs and how business increases and downturns could affect FTE counts.

Governance: The term "governance" is used to describe how the company is chartered to operate. It is normally an outcome of the companies by laws and regulations and prescribes the authorities and relationships between management the company's board.

Hiring Authority: That is the person who is going to hire you. That person probably will need to vet that decision with others, to include HR, but as the Hiring Authority you can expect that person will be your boss. It's useful to ask who it is if you are confused. I was surprised during one hiring process by mistaking what I thought was a potential future peer who instead turned out to be a potential future boss.

On-Boarding: The term used to describe how you are "in-processed" into the company. In many well-run companies it is a vital program that is designed to impart the company's values and culture, so do not assume that you can treat it lightly.

President and CEO: We often think of the term as interchangeable. They are not; a President normally leads an operating division. That person in turn reports to a Chief Executive Officer (CEO). The CEO reports to a Board. When the two titles are combined the job combines day to day leadership of a Company and reports directly to the Board. In exceptional circumstances the Chairman of the Board may also be CEO, but that is increasingly frowned upon by experts in corporate governance and accountability who want to diversify executive responsibility.

Profit and Loss (P&L): When you are offered a job, it is vital to learn whether it includes Profit and Loss responsibility or is strictly a staff job. Just like the military line commands versus staff, much greater importance is ascribed to P&L jobs because they are responsible for the financial success and performance of the company.

Recruiter: A firm or person normally hired by and organization to identify potential candidates for a job. Typically, a recruiting firm is responsible for developing the desired job description from specifications provided by the client. Then the recruiter uses that job description to develop candidates.

Rough Terrain Container Handler (RTCH): A RTCH is a 118-thousand-pound vehicle capable of transporting 20' or 40' commercial containers across unimproved surfaces. The RT240 RTCH is the US military standard vehicle and is made in Cibolo, Texas.

For the Civilian Audience

After Action Review (AAR): The Army conducts an After-Action Review following any major training event to ensure that key participants understood how their actions contributed to the outcome. The central aspect of this stylized process features an all-knowing Observer-Controller (OC) who has complete knowledge regarding what happened and ensures that all participants participate in a humble and truthful manner.

Counter Insurgency (COIN): Counter Insurgency warfare is the kind of warfare that the US has been forced to practice in Iraq and Afghanistan once the initial "kinetic" battles were complete. COIN focuses on hearts and minds instead of direct combat and casualties.

Director Programs, G8, and Director Force Development, Army Staff: The Army G-8 is the Army's lead for matching available resources to the defense strategy and the Army plan. The Director Force Development (FD) works as a subordinate of the G8 to design and execute the Army's equipping strategy.

Commissioned Officers, Warrant Officers and Senior Non-Commissioned Officers (NCO)s: Leaders in the military are identified by the source of their authority. A Commissioned Officer holds rank by a Commission, a Warrant Officer by virtue of a Warrant, and a Non-Commissioned Officer is appointed without a commission.

Military Retiree: A Servicemember typically is eligible for retirement following 20 years of active federal service. A medical retiree retires when his retirement disability is recognized. Reserve Component (Guard and Reserve) members typically retire later based on their years of Active and Reserve Service.

Steve Speakes is a proud Army Veteran with 35 years' service. Currently he is the President and CEO of a company making rough terrain equipment for the US Department of Defense and the commercial marketplace.

His final assignment was as a lieutenant general assigned as the Army's Deputy Chief of Staff for Programs, G8, retiring in 2009. Following his time in the military, Steve set out to become a businessman. His transition began with an opportunity to serve as USAA's Executive Vice President for Strategy and External Affairs. After three years in the job Steve was let go. Shortly afterwards he became the President and CEO of Kalmar Rough Terrain Center. After his second civilian job leading a small defense contractor, Steve shares the difficult lessons learned as a military retiree transitioning to the business world. As you will learn, success in his new life was difficult. Steve shares both what went wrong for him in a tough self-examination of his weaknesses, as well as describing how to "unlock" the secrets of the commercial world.

For transitioning military leaders this account has the courage to address real issues many transitioning retirees experience. For Civilian leaders, Steve suggests they study how to position Veterans for success in their organizations. As a Nation we all can learn from a candid look at this difficult subject.

Made in the USA
Columbia, SC
08 October 2024